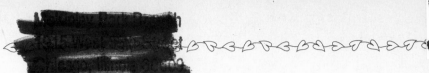

Using Beloved Classics to Deepen Reading Comprehension

RICH LESSONS AND LITERATURE RESPONSE ACTIVITIES THAT
IMPROVE KIDS' READING COMPREHENSION, BUILD WRITING
SKILL... ...D EVERY READER

NEW YOR... ...CKLAND • SYDNEY
MEXICO CITY • NEW DELHI • HONG KONG • BUENOS AIRES

Dedication

To all my students

Acknowledgments

It was my fantasy as a child to see my name on a book when I grew up. I became a teacher and enjoyed focusing my creative energies in my classroom, never expecting my dream to come true. It did, in 1994, when I first met Terry Cooper, who encouraged me to write the first edition of this book. She and Wendy Murray suggested this new edition, for which I am very grateful. It has been a pleasure to work with them and everyone else at Scholastic.

In 1990, at an NEH summer seminar at Princeton University, Professor Ulrich C. Knoepflmacher introduced me to a whole new way of looking at children's literature. I went back to my classroom that fall and tried some of it out with my own students and was delighted to find them as excited as I had been. Since then I've received several more NEH fellowships allowing me to study with other scholars including Judy Pasamanick, Jack Zipes, and Russell Peck.

For some years now I've been a member of two Internet discussion groups on children's literature: Child_lit and Ccbcnet. I've been incredibly fortunate in making many friends through these two groups— children's book writers, teachers, librarians, editors, and more. Every time I log on I learn something new from them.

Thank you to the children, parents, colleagues, staff, and administration at the Dalton School, who have been unfailingly supportive of my work. And lastly, I thank my family, who have inspired me to write and enjoy literature every day.

Cover design by Josué Castilleja
Interior design by Grafica, Inc.
Cover and interior photographs by Joan Beard

ISBN 0-439-27860-0

Table of Contents

Introduction

Kids like to dig. On the beach. In the backyard. Through cluttered bedrooms. And when they do, what treasures they discover! A beautiful shell. A wiggly worm. A forgotten toy.

This is a book about helping children dig deep into literature. I've been doing this with fourth graders for over 10 years now and each year has been better than the last. It has been wonderful watching my students' excitement as they uncover new riches through their literary investigations.

Instead of a beautiful seashell, they discover E. B. White's exquisite prose. Instead of a wiggly worm, they meet the real Alice Liddell, who inspired Lewis Carroll to write *Alice's Adventures in Wonderland*. And the children realize that Cinderella is no kindergarten relic, but a most sophisticated young lady. Delving into these texts and others, my students find literary treasures every day.

Digging deep into literature helps children with many aspects of their learning. I've seen them become more fluent readers, more able decoders, and more confident at comprehension—all as a result of these literary explorations. Their writing improves as students are inspired and stimulated by the range of activities and materials.

This book will introduce you to the possibilities of a classroom where teachers and children work *together* to dig deep into literature. I have included background information on folktales, fairy tales, novels, and authors as well as practical language arts activities to use with your own class. My approach is thematic and multidimensional, embracing reading, writing, speaking, and the visual and performing arts. The units are tried and true; I have developed and used them with elementary students over a number of years. While my experience has been mainly with fourth graders, the units are adaptable for younger and older students. Use the ideas in this book as a stepping-off point, and change and mold them to fit your style of teaching and your students' particular needs.

Digging Deep into Literature: What's It All About?

"Imagination is more important than knowledge."

—ALBERT EINSTEIN,
"ON SCIENCE"

B ooks have always been the cornerstones of my existence. I have rarely run the briefest errand without bringing along a book, and I am happiest on vacation with hours free to read. When I was a child, the highlight of my week was my visit to the library, where I took out as many books as I could carry home. Once I even attempted to copy a much beloved book by hand. (I managed three chapters, but eventually had to return the book or risk losing borrowing privileges.) I treasured the books I owned, and family and friends always knew that the perfect gift for me was a book.

My passion for reading and books has been something I have always communicated to my students throughout my many years of teaching.

My other lives include Peace Corps volunteer, world traveler, writer, artist, and computer maven, all of which have contributed to my growth as a teacher. In 1990 yet another new life opened for me at Princeton University, where, as a National Endowment for the Humanties Fellow, I studied children's literature with Professor Ulrich Knoepflmacher. This life as a literary scholar was a new experience for me, studying children's literature with the same degree of seriousness that others do Shakespeare. There I was discoursing on the meaning of *Charlotte's Web* at the seminar table and examining rare copies of *Alice in Wonderland* in the library. I returned to my classroom that September excited about helping my student have a similar experience. Why couldn't they be literary scholars as I had been? I thought.

And before long they were, digging deep into literature.

DIGGING DEEP INTO LITERATURE

y digging deep into literature I mean doing the sort of work scholars do. Children, I've discovered, love to grapple with demanding ideas. Going beyond the basic story to probe more deeply is very exciting for them. It doesn't necessarily demand high-level readers either. Some of the best discussions about literature that I've had with students were based on books I'd read aloud to them. Digging deep into literature means looking hard at writing, at the times in which a book was written, at many other aspects of the book and the author. It means staying with a book, a story, or a poem for some time. It means close reading, rereading, and thinking hard about a piece of literature. It is an approach that I find stimulating as a teacher and that my students find engaging and exciting. And I've seen that when my students are motivated and engaged they learn more about everything!

Your students don't have to be super readers to dig deep into literature. In fact, year after year some of the most sophisticated comments have come from those students who are still struggling with basic reading and writing skills. What this approach provides is a stimulating way for all readers, whatever their ability, to investigate literature and improve their comprehension skills at the same time.

CHILDREN AS LITERARY EXPERTS

y students come to me with varying degrees of abilities, comfort, and attitudes about reading. Their previous school experiences have ranged from whole language to traditional classrooms. Some are avid readers and throw themselves into books. Others struggle, still locked into decoding issues, insecure and negative about books. My challenge is to create a learning environment that excites and empowers everyone.

Promoting the idea that we all can be literary experts helps to build a classroom community. Language arts skills such as reading, writing, listening, and speaking are all easy to nurture within such a literature-based program. Since my class is heterogeneous, I am careful to vary whole-class, small-group, and individual book study. I also balance teacher-selected versus student-selected reading materials. Individual conferences and group discussions on specific reading strategies are ways in which I help those with difficulties. I give tremendous emphasis to personal response and interpretation, and often tie writing directly to reading via journal entries, fiction written in response to reading, and research report writing.

READER RESPONSE

ne way to help children become literary experts is to use a reader-response approach to literature. Louise M. Rosenblatt, a pioneer in this field, describes two types of reading: aesthetic and efferent. An aesthetic reading is personal; each person brings his or her own experiences to the text and each of these transactions is unique. My *Charlotte's Web* will be very different from your *Charlotte's Web*. At the other end of the continuum is the efferent stance: reading for information. Skimming the daily newspaper is a good example of efferent reading. Aesthetic and efferent approaches can occur at the same time. "We read for information, but we are also conscious of emotions about it and feel pleasure when the words we call

up arouse vivid images that are rhythmic to the inner ear. Or we experience a poem but are conscious of acquiring some information about, say, Greek warfare. To confuse matters even further, we can switch stances while reading. Our present purpose and past experiences, as well as the text are factors in our choice of stance" (Rosenblatt, 1991, p. 445).

Reader response encourages my students to value their own experiences with books and to learn that it is possible for everyone in the class to have a different interpretation of the same book, all equally valid. Once they understand this they can begin to approach books as scholars, returning to the text to see what else is in it, considering how it compares to other books, to real life, to anything else they wish to explore.

INDEPENDENT READING

y students select their own books for a nightly reading assignment and respond to these readings in class discussions and in a journal. I require that the children read 30 minutes a night; parents are helpful in seeing that this is accomplished. Often students need help choosing the right books, finding the right place to read, and sticking with the task for the full 30 minutes. Sometimes parents use a timer to see that the 30 minutes of reading is accounted for; others plan a timetable of specific chapters and pages. As I get to know my students, I am able to work in a partnership with each one and his or her parents to help them become better readers. For some students, all I have to do is pull a book off a shelf in our classroom library and say, "I think you would really enjoy this book." For others it can be a more difficult quest to find the right book and the right way to read at home. Sometimes a student may need to try several books and many different authors until one really clicks. I encourage students to stop reading books they don't like. I see no reason why a student should struggle through to the end of a book she hates, especially if reading is an unpleasant activity for her in the first place.

LITERATURE STUDIES

I have created a series of thematic units built around books that I love and that I feel are valuable to know. My students become literary experts, examining these books and authors closely. This can mean researching an author's life, discovering historical information relevant to the book, or even reading literary criticism if there is interest. The idea of studying and responding to literature as a communal experience is an important element of the program. These students are not solitary scholars, each isolated in his or her own ivory tower. Their ideas, responses, and interpretations expand as they interact with each other, with me, and with the text.

MODELING LITERARY EXPERTISE

In my classroom, I am the experienced reader and scholar. My role is to express passion and enthusiasm for literature, to demonstrate how to think deeply about books, and to nudge and bring out similar behaviors in my students. I have had time to develop a critical stance while my students come to me as neophytes, amazed that there is more to reading a book than simply getting the main ideas. Teachers are literary experts already and need to model what that means for their students. "Teachers are the leading critics in the classroom; they point the way

to searching out the potential of a text" (Peterson and Eeds, 1990, p. 23). My students value my expertise even as they develop their own.

CREATING A CLASSROOM READING COMMUNITY

My students are used to a clearly defined system of weaker, stronger, and strongest readers. It is a struggle to get them to consider everyone as part of the same community of readers. They know which members of the class are avid readers who read a book a day and which ones struggle to get through a page a day. Some stumble along when reading orally, yet understand beautifully when left to read on their own. Others can decode every word, yet understand little of the subtleties of the text. Students quickly figure out "school" and have rock-solid ideas as to what constitutes a good or bad reader. For them it has more to do with speed and accuracy than with personal response and interpretation.

To begin building a community of readers, I give my students a letter like the one shown on page 13 during the first week of school. We read and discuss it together.

Creating a whole-class community of readers is a way of breaking down the students' stereotypes of good and bad readers. I expect everyone to be responsible and capable of participating in our literature studies. For example, I put the responsibility on the children to decide how long they need to complete a book rather than impose my own deadlines for them. Starting the year with a book like *Charlotte's Web* helps to quickly solidify the community. It is so well liked and well known that my fourth graders all feel confident expressing their feelings about it to the group and to me in their journals.

Dear Readers,

I would like to welcome you to our fourth-grade reading club and tell you about what you can expect to be doing in Reading Workshop this year. I love to read and have been reading for a long time. But I didn't always love reading. I spent second grade in Germany. When I started school in Germany, I didn't like reading at all. This was a problem because I was learning to read German at school and English at home (with my mother). At some point that year something clicked and I began to like reading. My favorite book (which I have here in school) was *My Naughty Little Sister*. I also have my German reading book from that year. Ever since then I have loved reading and have read all kinds of things, everything from Nancy Drew mysteries to *Tom Sawyer*.

I am sure you all have different feelings about reading. Some of you may love it, some may think it is okay, some may think it is boring, some may absolutely hate it. Well, whatever you think about reading, it is something you need to do well because you will be doing it a lot in your life! There are so many reasons to read, and I hope that you will all identify many of them this year.

We will generally have Reading Workshop every day. There will be two aspects to the Reading Workshop. One part will involve your independent reading and the other will involve group literature study. You will not be assigned permanent reading groups. Some of your work will be independent, some in small groups, some with the whole class. The groups will change and be determined in different ways: by book choice, by numbering off, by who works well together, by talkers and listeners.

You will be expected to always have an independent reading book in school and for homework. You are expected to read this book at least 30 minutes every night and to bring it to school every day. Once a week you will be required to write about this book in your reading journal. I will write responses to your journal entries. I need to be able to read these entries, but you should not worry about spelling or punctuation. I am more interested in what you write than how it looks. You may read whatever you wish. Your parents, classmates, the librarians, and I will be most willing to suggest books to read. In addition to writing about your reading in a journal, you will have conferences with me about your reading and, at times, discuss your reading in class meetings.

The other part of Reading Workshop will be literature study. We will be studying authors and their books as a class. You will be working as literary experts, studying books as do people in universities and colleges. For example, our first major study will be on E. B. White and our first book, *Charlotte's Web.* Many of you will already know White's books, but, believe me, this will be a new and different way of looking at them!

I love to read, love children's literature, and love leading literature studies. Every year it is so exciting to watch my class become a community of readers, learning to appreciate what everyone has to offer in the reading of a book.

Welcome to a wonderful, exciting year of reading and literature!

Ms. Edinger

In order to develop a true reading community I feel that I must help children move away from a good/bad view of readers. This idea needs to be reaffirmed throughout the year. With every new unit, I am careful to stress the importance of deep understanding and personal response over speed and informational reading.

DISCUSSIONS

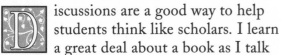iscussions are a good way to help students think like scholars. I learn a great deal about a book as I talk with others about it in a group. "Learning what others have made of a text can greatly increase such insight into one's own relationship with it. A reader who has been moved or disturbed by a text often manifests an urge to talk about it, to clarify and crystallize his sense of the work. He likes to hear others' views. Through such interchange he can discover how people bringing different temperaments, different literary and life experiences to the text have engaged in very different transactions with it" (Rosenblatt, 1976, p. 146).

Functioning as a discussion leader is one of the hardest things I do as a teacher. Generally, I begin with the question "What did you think of the book?" and move the discussion on from the initial responses. I must encourage all ideas, see that no one child or gender dominates the discussion, get everyone to participate, affirm the literal as well as the more abstract idea, know when to sit back and listen and when to step in, model confusion with a passage or chapter, encourage disagreement as a way of struggling with deeper meaning, move the discussion on with a new thought if necessary, pick up on ideas that demand more thought, and try throughout to observe my students' process. It is quite a juggling act! Yet, I have concluded after years of observation and contemplation about my role that I must be there, actively leading the discussion for the ideas to bubble up, be recognized, and be examined.

JOURNALS

ournals are another means for my students and me to interact around a text. These are personal journals, also known as response journals, dialogue journals, or learning logs. Their purpose is to provide a private place for students to write responses to their reading and for me to respond to them. When it works well, the journal becomes a private conversation between me and the student. At first, students respond to their independent reading. To help them get started, I read responses from former students and give them a list of response ideas, some from experts like Nancie Atwell; others, ideas that students and I have come up with over the years. The tendency is for responses to be plot summaries. As the year goes on, I am able to move most students away from these into more thoughtful responses. I have journal readings when each student selects a favorite entry to read to the class. Once we are involved in a literature study I will often ask students to respond to a specific book or film. Some students are able to express themselves more honestly in a journal while others, being more verbal, prefer the discussions.

The journal is a good way for students to distinguish between writing to learn and writing for publication. I see the journals as reflective writing, primarily used to learn more. My responses to students' entries have to be as sensitive as my responses are in discussions. My students need to feel we are having a private dialogue and look forward to reading my responses as much as I look forward to reading theirs. Just as a student can find too many questions from me tedious, so can I let them know when they have bored me with endless plot summaries.

As the year goes on, we are able to begin comparing and contrasting books. After our *Cinderella* study, for example, students will constantly refer to it in their journals. They love comparing characters from different books, trying to see similarities and differences. Different classes have different interests. One year, I had a group that watched a great deal of television and brought that into their book discussions. Another group enjoyed writing letters on behalf of characters. Of course I had to answer the character, and not the student!

Every year I find journals to be a more powerful teaching tool. At first I called them "reading journals," but now I call them "response journals." That way we can use them to respond to whatever we wish. I use them for spontaneous responses to current events and to classroom problems, as well as to academic materials.

At the end of every year I ask the students to read through their journals and then write one final letter to me reflecting on their growth as readers and writers during the year.

Jonathan's final reflections letter

Dear Ms. Edinger,

Thank you for the best year I ever had! We had the coolest projects and lots of fun. My favorite was *Alice*. I loved writing a funny parody and illustrating it. Then came oral history. I loved the interview and turning it into a book. Then came Pilgrims. And thanks for recommending *The Golden Compass*. Now it's my favorite book!

I think I learned a lot about writing. More detail, less "I liked this." "I liked that." I use more analogies, compare more things, use better vocabulary. I learned different ways of writing. I used to write just uptight.

I have learned to read a variety of books, not just powerful ones. I read a lot harder books. I read more and, most of all, enjoy the books a lot more.

Thanks again for my favorite year.

Sincerely,

Jonathan

ORAL READINGS

When I first began teaching fourth grade at my current school, we had homogeneous reading groups and I had my students read aloud every day. I was sure that it helped with comprehension, and it reassured me that they were all decoding correctly. Since we eliminated reading groups several years ago, students have made clear to me how much they disliked oral reading and how it only confused them rather than helped them. It helped me realize that fluent oral reading does not necessarily make for perfect comprehension or vice versa. Therefore, I eliminated round-robin reading and emphasized silent reading.

One year I asked students to prepare favorite readings to present during our morning meetings. Two or three students read aloud every morning at the close of our meeting. Students loved explaining why they had selected a particular part of a book and read with wonderful expression and enjoyment. Their classmates equally enjoyed listening. What made it different from round-robin readings was that this time the students decided what to read and had a chance to practice beforehand. We weren't doing it to be sure everyone understood. We were doing it to hear what they liked. It made the experience completely different and enjoyable for all.

Serendipitously, poetry readings also have become part of our day. I run a very brief class meeting before dismissal where homework and issues of the day are discussed. One day a student came in with a book of Robert Frost's poetry and said she had been reading some of the poems with her father and wanted to read one to the class. I suggested she do so at the end of the day. The next day another student brought in a poem to read, and before long we had established the end-of-day meeting as a time for poetry. I brought in a variety of poetry books and students searched the library for favorites. One of the most impressive was a boy who did a remarkable reading of Poe's "The Raven" without any practice. There is no doubt that end-of-day poetry readings will become a permanent ritual in my classroom from now on.

WRITING

PERSONAL WRITING

Personal writing is the reflective, intimate kind that takes place in response journals. This is writing to learn, to muse and speculate. My students write to me in their journals with the understanding that I only wish to know more about their thinking. I make it clear that as long as I can read what they have written, handwriting and spelling do not matter.

PUBLIC WRITING

Public writing is for publication. Parents, teachers, and peers can all be readers of public writing. It can be a poem, a report, a story, or a poster. The important thing is that there is an understanding on the author's part that others will read this piece of writing. This means that drafts and revisions are an important part of the process of writing for publication. My students publish regularly: research journals, informational handbooks, book reviews, poetry posters, memoir books, and story collections.

Writing workshop in my class is a daily affair. I begin with mini-lessons based on the needs of my students and then have them write for the bulk of the period. Students confer with me and each other as they write and revise their pieces. The idea of multiple drafts is an important one for my students. Skills are taught in context:

Quotation marks, for example, become a mini-lesson topic when students are writing a lot of dialogue and find the skill useful. Whole-class response sessions are a regular part of the workshop. In 1984 I attended Lucy McCormick Calkin's Writing Institute at Teachers College Columbia University and have continued to learn about process writing through conferences, journals, workshops, and books. The writings of Donald Graves and Nancie Atwell have been especially influential in helping me grow as a writing teacher.

PROJECTS

One of students' favorite ways to respond to literature is through projects. These are nothing new. I remember doing dioramas and posters when I was a child. They are still an excellent way for children to create an original and personal response to literature.

Numerous books exists with fine project ideas. Students love to write sequels and parodies, poems, and plays based on favorite works of literature. My students have done skits, puppet shows, raps, videos, and meals as projects. We have done whole-class projects such as plays, murals, or magazines. Sometimes everyone works in groups and sometimes everyone works alone. Presenting projects is important. Students are thrilled to invite another class or, best of all, family members to a project presentation.

FINAL THOUGHTS

Elementary students are capable of great interpretive depths when analyzing literature. Encouraging them to dig deep into a book empowers them. If you encourage them to think of themselves as literary experts they will think more highly of themselves as readers and writers. My students come in all shapes and sizes. Some read at adult levels while others are still struggling with making meaning out of the simplest text. However, every single one of them has been able to delve into books as do literary scholars. And they learn that being a good reader is far more than getting the words right, reading quickly, or getting the facts. They learn that it is about reaching beyond the words to the author's meaning, to theme and character, to emotion and more. At the start of the year I model for them a passion for reading and analyzing literature. By the end of the year my students are passionate literary scholars themselves, digging deep into literature.

Digging Deep with Authors: A Study of E. B. White

"I haven't told why I wrote the book, but I haven't told why I sneeze, either. A book is a sneeze."

—E. B. WHITE ON *CHARLOTTE'S WEB*

My sister and I frequently dressed our stoical cat in doll clothes and wheeled her about in a carriage. She was the baby in our games of House. Had our dogs been smaller and more cooperative I have no doubt we would have found roles for them, perhaps as beasts of burden or as additional family members. Stuffed animals also served as participants in a wide range of games. We provided them with food and clothing and used them in elaborate stories. My teddy bear stood by me when I was sent to my room, understood when everyone else was being unfair, and protected me against all the evils of the night.

Animals have a special place in our childhood. Perhaps it is their vulnerability, their reliance on us that parallels our needs as children. How else to explain the delight we take in animal stories, especially talking animal stories. Life in these books seems so real: The main characters act, feel, and suffer as human beings. Often they live in towns, hold jobs, or go to school. Even if the setting is an animal habitat, the characters in this genre act and speak as humans.

Certainly, a master of this genre was E. B. White. His three children's books, all featuring talking animals, are classics of children's literature. There is a timelessness to them that keeps them beloved by generation upon generation of children. A master writer and editor, White was meticulous about his work. An author study of E. B. White, centered around *Stuart Little*, *Charlotte's Web*, and *The Trumpet of the Swan*, can be a fine way to help children appreciate what the art of writing is all about. It can also be a gentle entry into the world of fantasy literature.

DIGGING DEEP WITH AN AUTHOR STUDY

've found that one of the best ways to introduce the idea of digging deep into literature is with an author study. Taking a look at one author's work provides us with a way of looking more deeply at how a writer works. While there are many living authors who are often featured in author studies, I recommend investigating authors from the past as well. Authors of well-known classics often are less familiar to students yet fascinating to study. I've also found it fun as a teacher to see what sort of material is available about a particular author. The Internet has made it remarkably easy to find out quite a lot.

STARTING THE YEAR WITH E. B. WHITE

or some time now I've been starting my fourth graders' year with an author study of E. B. White. I begin the school year with this unit for several reasons. My students generally are already familiar with White's children's stories, and re-experiencing them is comforting at a time when everything else is so new. Not only are my fourth graders beginning a new school year with a new teacher and a new class, but they are also in a new building as the first grade of our middle school. To make it even harder, our high school is in the same building. It is truly frightening for many of my small charges to move through the stairwells and halls, alternately ignored, teased, or belittled by their far older and larger schoolmates. It is easy for them to sympathize with Stuart's difficulties or identify with Wilbur, the runt of his litter.

Another reason to begin the year with E. B. White is that there is no better writer to present to children when teaching about the writing process. White was one of the most accomplished writers and editors of this century. His enduring popularity ensures that there will always be plenty of material about his life and his writing, and especially about the writing of his children's books. Students realize that the magic of *Charlotte's Web* came from White's love of nature, in-depth research, pondering, and careful craftsmanship as a writer. It is a lesson that will stay with them forever.

White's books are also a very gentle introduction to fantasy literature. They hardly seem like other kinds of fantasy literature since the settings are so realistically rendered. I taught these books for years without thinking of them as fantasy literature. It was only when I began to think seriously about what fantasy literature was that I realized that talking animals like Stuart, Charlotte, and Louise belonged to the genre. These kinds of realistic talking-animal stories are sometimes referred to as low-fantasy while those with magic and imaginary lands are termed high-fantasy. I have found that talking-animal stories often appeal to students who dislike the higher types of fantasy literature.

CHARLOTTE'S WEB: A WHOLE CLASS READING A WHOLE BOOK TOGETHER

I begin the unit with a whole-class study of *Charlotte's Web*. I do this because I simply think the book is one of the most perfect books ever written, and my students invariably agree with me. *Charlotte's Web* was actually White's second children's book, a middle child, written after *Stuart Little* and before *The Trumpet of the Swan*.

To begin, I seat my class in a circle on the floor of our meeting area and give students paperback copies of their own. I tell them that we will be studying the book as scholars do and that they will want to mark up the book with their own ideas— ending up with a very personal *Charlotte's Web*. I show them my marked-up, well-thumbed copy as an example. We discuss previous experiences with the book. For many, it was read aloud to them. Others know the story from the animated film. A smaller number may have read it in school or on their own. Once in a while I come across a neophyte and envy his or her pleasure as a first-timer. In the course of the discussion, I introduce the idea of multiple readings of a book. This is a new idea for fourth graders. So many are still uncertain about reading; it is hard work for them and not always pleasurable. Reading a chapter book all the way through is a feat for many,

and the idea of rereading is revolutionary. Yet *Charlotte's Web* is so beloved that even the most reluctant readers are willing to approach it for the first, second, or umpteenth time. I tell them that I read it at least once every year (when they do) and enjoy it each time.

The idea that everyone in the class will be reading the same book is often new to many of my students. Their previous school reading experiences have tended to be in small groups. Often, the reading ability in the class ranges from those who can read the book in a couple of hours to those who need several weeks to complete it. I acknowledge this situation to the whole class immediately. They need to recognize this range among themselves and be sensitive and helpful to each other. We negotiate a date when everyone in the class feels they can be finished with the book. Generally, I have found that three weeks is a reasonable time for all. The book has 22 chapters, so a slow reader can plan to read approximately one chapter a day to meet such a deadline. Since I also have an independent reading program, children who finish quickly can continue with books of their own choice. For these students, the fear is that they will have forgotten the book in two weeks, since they are used to reading small amounts and discussing it immediately within a reading group. It is another small lesson for these high achievers to realize that it is possible to read a book and still remember it weeks later (if, like *Charlotte's Web*, it is worth remembering).

I provide enough daily reading time so that everyone has plenty of time to finish the book. While I enjoy informal conversations about the book as students are reading it, I do not run formal whole-group discussions until everyone has finished. For years I taught reading by chapters. That is, I assigned a chapter to read and we discussed it the next day. I was always frustrated because I knew the whole book, but I couldn't discuss anything past the chapter we were on. Invariably, there were others in the group who had also read further. It always struck me as a very artificial way to approach a book, and I have done away with it completely.

Certainly, my students are welcome to talk to each other and to me as they read the book. And they do. I listen to them read bits aloud that they like and discuss how they cried when Charlotte died. I watch those who become so absorbed in the book that it takes three calls from me until they look up and realize that it is time for gym. Weekly journal entries are all about the book: what they feel about it, who they like and don't like, and (for first-timers) what they think will happen next.

FIRST RESPONSE DISCUSSIONS

When everyone is finished with the book, we meet as a whole class to give initial reactions. This is a very free-flowing discussion. I simply begin by asking, "What did you think of the book?" Invariably, someone will have something to say, which will give someone else an idea, and the discussion will be underway. I am strict about respect and courtesy. I am the discussion leader and require that everyone listen respectfully and raise his or her hand in order to speak. If there are many hands in the air I will call on several students, "First Mary, then Jon, then Nancy, and then David." Running such a discussion with a large group is difficult. However, I feel that these discussions need to be with the whole class. It is still the beginning of the year and these students need to become a group. Discussing *Charlotte's Web* as a whole class is a way towards that goal. Class members need to hear each other's ideas and learn that Mary, who took three weeks to finish the book, has some of the

most profound thoughts on the book. Mary also needs to realize that, despite being a slow reader, she has much to offer to the group when it comes time to discuss the book. It also helps me to learn about them; that Jon likes to raise his hand whether or not he has something to say, or that Sarah needs to be lauded on the rare occasion she does speak up.

STUDYING *CHARLOTTE'S WEB* UP CLOSE

Once sufficient time has been devoted to personal responses to the book, I introduce the idea of annotation and close reading of a text. By annotating I mean writing notes directly into the book, and by close reading I mean studying a text line by line. Doing this with a few pages of a book as carefully and beautifully written as *Charlotte's Web* can be an eye-opening experience for students. I show the class my own well-marked copy of *Charlotte's Web* as well as examples of published works such as *The Annotated Charlotte's Web*. I then explain to them that scholars do close readings of books and that we will be doing this with *Charlotte's Web*. While it is enjoyable to simply read a book for its story, it can also be interesting to dig deeper into a book and study what the author had in mind as he or she wrote it, how the author wrote it, and, perhaps, why.

A Close Reading of Chapter 1

I demonstrate a close reading with Chapter 1. I show students where I have underlined and made notes at certain places in the text. My initial close reading was done with Professor Ulrich Knoepflmacher during my NEH Summer Seminar at Princeton University, but subsequent readings alone and with students have caused me to add notes. Significant points in this first chapter are the references to death and the contrast between Fern's agitation and her mother and father's calm. White's wonderful descriptions are evident immediately, especially his description of a breakfast of bacon. Thus White immediately makes clear the point of a pig on a farm: to produce bacon. Fern's brother Avery is also introduced, a contrast to the pacifistic Fern with his air rifle and wooden dagger. The chapter ends with Fern naming Wilbur. The connection to the author (White) with Wilbur (also "white") can be made.

To help focus on the life/death imagery, I create a chart and ask the students to look for words referring to life or death in the first chapter.

CHAPTER 1	
Life	**Death**
born	do away
springtime	die
love	kill
morning light	air rifle
breakfast	wooden dagger

We also investigate all the names to see if they have additional significance. For example, Arable means "plowable" and Fern is a plant. It is interesting to consider what White had in mind with names like Lurvy, Homer Zuckerman, Dr. Dorian, and Henry Fussy. (In the film, Henry is indeed a fussy child, but that does not come across in the book at all. His main role seems to be to draw Fern into adulthood and away from the barn.) It is fun to wonder how White selected names like Wilbur and Charlotte, solid "Americana" names.

Annotating *Charlotte's Web*

Once I have completed modeling how to do a close reading of Chapter 1, each student selects one chapter to study. Since I usually have classes of 20 or 21, this means one chapter per student. If I had a larger class I would encourage students to double up on certain, longer chapters. Each reader negotiates a deadline with me.

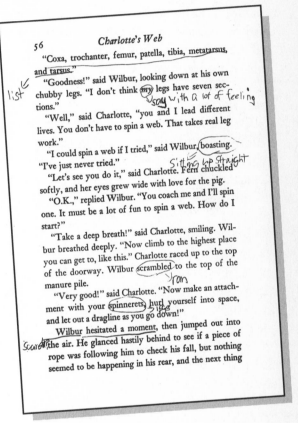

A page from a student's annotation of Charlotte's Web

The chapter annotations take time. I tend to do them in two long class sessions, but other teachers who have used the unit prefer to conduct three or four shorter sessions. Each group will have its own temperament and need to be considered differently. It is a time-consuming, lengthy process, but most worthwhile. My role is to help the reporter along. Each student needs to feel like an expert on his/her chapter, yet it is also important not to lose the rest of the class if one reader is going tediously through every line of the chapter. Sometimes, to speed things up, I ask them to report on one thing per page.

Students frequently note White's delightful descriptive passages. They note his love of smells and his frequent references to manure. They love his lists, especially the lists of Wilbur's meals. Often they note the change in point of view. At times the voice of the narrator (White) overrides that of the characters. They enjoy noting the shift in tone from reminiscences of summer days to the more direct dialogue of the barn animals.

One student, highly insecure about her reading ability, found a gem in the chapter where Charlotte dies. She noted that just as Charlotte dies alone in the midst of the fair, so she dies in the middle of the paragraph.

Our Class Notes for *Charlotte's Web*

I realized, after doing this unit for a number of years, that many students were attempting to write every note from every chapter report in their own books. At times this slowed down the presentations, since students were novices at this sort of note-taking. Yet, I was delighted that they wanted to do this, to fill their books with their own and their classmates' ideas about this book. My solution was our own self-published endnotes for our personal copies of *Charlotte's Web*. This appendix ended up consisting of one page for each chapter. I showed the students how some books, rather than having annotations on the actual pages of the text or footnotes, placed these notes at the end of the book in an appendix of notes. A colleague, Julia Stokien, created a form that made it simple for each student to select the highlights of his or her chapter notes. Additionally, there was a place below for other students to add notes, as I had noticed that some especially enthusiastic readers had annotated other chapters in addition to their own.

Here is Josh's chart of notes for Chapter 21, "The Egg Sac." (See one of his annotated pages of the book on page 23.)

Josh's Notes for *Charlotte's Web*

	Chapter # 21	Chapter Title <u>The Egg Sac</u>

Page	Quote	Note
145	"…and the early automobiles went whispering along the road."	White is very descriptive.
146	"Plaything? I should say not. It is my egg sac, my magnum opus."	White did a lot of research for *Charlotte's Web*.
145	"Yes, it is pretty," replied Charlotte.	Charlotte is always so modest.
146	"I think I'm languishing to tell you the truth."	Life/death. Is Charlotte afraid to say, "dying"?
147	"His stomach was as big around as a jelly jar."	Very descriptive.
148	"You might as well relax—nobody is going to hang a medal on you."	Foreshadowing.
149	"Wilbur and Charlotte were glad to get rid of him for a while."	Sounds like me about my sister sometimes.
150	"Tears came to Fern's eyes."	Why is she so sad?
151	"Avery kissed Wilbur."	Avery is not his usual self.
153	"'Put that buttermilk into the truck!' commanded Mr. Arable. Avery grabbed the jar and rushed to the truck."	Avery is actually listening to his parents.
154	"As they passed the Ferris wheel, Fern gazed up at it and wished she were in the top most car with Henry Fussy at her side."	Fern changes. She used to love Wilbur so much. Now she's into Henry Fussy.

QUESTIONS TO PONDER

Over the years that I have taught this unit I have always asked students to answer the following questions:

> *Who is the hero and why do you think so?*
>
> *Who is selfish and why do you think so?*

These two simple questions have provoked some of the most heated discussions regarding the book. Generally, the greatest disagreement is over considering Fern and/or Charlotte heroes. In the course of the discussion we start to define heroism. My students have tended to argue that heroism means saving a life. I have even had students argue that Templeton is a hero for bringing back the egg sac! For many, there is the feeling that Fern deserted Wilbur and thus lost her right to be heroic. Others feel she is still the hero for saving Wilbur in the first place. The question always provokes thought and has never produced a dull discussion. The question of selfishness is also one that animates the whole group. Middle-grade students are just moving out of a self-involved childhood state themselves, so they are very sensitive to the idea of selfishness. While Wilbur would seem the most likely candidate for most selfish, Templeton is up there too, as is Homer Zuckerman. See one class's notes on page 27.

THE REWRITING OF CHARLOTTE'S WEB

The Annotated Charlotte's Web with Peter Neumeyer's notes and Scott Elledge's *E. B. White: A Biography* are excellent resources for exploring White's process in writing the book. Both have copies of pages in different drafts, White's notes on spiders, a drawing of the barn, etc. It is particularly interesting

to examine the way White kept changing the beginning of the book. Fern did not exist in the earliest drafts; rather, the book began in the barn. It is fascinating to observe White revising and revising until later drafts begin to look like the beginning of the book we know today. Students are always deeply impressed with all the revising White did, and it invariably helps them to see the value of revision in their own work. If a great writer like E. B. White did so much, then they can too!

STUART LITTLE AND THE TRUMPET OF THE SWAN: SMALL GROUP STUDIES

 ask students to select either *Stuart Little* or *The Trumpet of the Swan* for their second White book. I try to see to it that the groups are balanced in terms of numbers, but that is all. My experience has been that students are truly interested in reading one or the other and do not make a decision based on one book being "easier" or because a friend will be in a particular group. I do not go into as detailed a study with these two books as I do with *Charlotte's Web*. The purpose here is to compare White's other books to *Charlotte's Web*.

The *Stuart Little* group often complains about the open-ended final chapter. They want Stuart to find Margalo. White intended it to be Stuart's journey into life, but my students don't always like this decision. Often, their frustration causes them to write new endings to the book that are more satisfactory to them.

One of the most interesting discussions about *The Trumpet of the Swan* concerned the way Louis negotiated Serena's freedom by offering one of their offspring to the zoo. My students were outraged that Louis did not consult Serena about the deal. They

Charlotte's Web:
HEROES
OUR OPINIONS

Charlotte because:
- ❀ She saved Wilbur's life by making the webs without anyone noticing her.
- ❀ From the beginning when we first meet Charlotte in the book she was Wilbur's friend.
- ❀ She is always helping Wilbur.
- ❀ The last line of the book tells it all, "...a true friend and a good writer. Charlotte was both."

Fern because:
- ❀ She saved Wilbur's life.
- ❀ She raised him like his mother.
- ❀ She cared for him.
- ❀ She visited him.

Wilbur because:
- ❀ He saved the egg sac.
- ❀ He won the award at the fair.
- ❀ He saved the egg sac for Charlotte.

Templeton because:
- ❀ He found the words for the web.
- ❀ He bit Wilbur's tale at a critical point without being bribed for once.

Lurvy because:
- ❀ He fed Wilbur.

Old Sheep because:
- ❀ She convinced Templeton to warn Wilbur.

Mr. Arable because:
- ❀ He kept Wilbur even though he was a runt.

To be a hero means to:
- ❀ Take risks
- ❀ Save lives
- ❀ Not be out for him/herself
- ❀ Be an exceptional being (such as a writing spider)
- ❀ Be brave

were horrified that Louis could give up a child so casually. Issues of adoption and foster care came up. Students were passionate and articulate.

During this part of the unit, I ask each student to select a favorite passage from *Stuart Little* or *The Trumpet of the Swan* to prepare as a reading to the class. Every morning two or three students read aloud their passages. Students enjoy this assignment. They take tremendous care with their choices and practice well ahead of time. Their classmates listen engrossed. We always discover some very fine readers through this assignment, and some quiet students turn out to be dramatic readers.

E. B. WHITE PROJECTS: BRINGING IT ALL TOGETHER

The final part of the unit is the project section. The students work alone or in groups to prepare a project that pulls together all their learning about E. B. White and his children's books. These projects are done as homework and presented on a day mutually agreed upon.

Some students enjoy performance projects. One year I had several video interviews of characters in all the books. Wilbur usually was played by a stuffed animal and several times Stuart was played by a pet gerbil. One year, a student created a video/puppet fantasy entitled "E. B. White in Paris." She had White meeting characters from his books as he traveled around Paris. Yet another student spent hours on a Claymation™ video involving characters from all three books.

FINAL THOUGHTS

 n author study of E. B. White is an excellent way to begin the school year and to start teaching students how to dig deep into literature. I have found that the tools of literary analysis that students first discover during this unit stay with them all year. They constantly refer to White and his children's book worlds. They remember what it is to annotate, what irony and foreshadowing are, and they use these techniques and ideas in other book discussions as the year goes on. This unit always makes my students feel like true literary scholars, capable of digging deep into any book they choose.

White's wonderful books *Charlotte's Web*, *Stuart Little*, and *The Trumpet of the Swan* are children's classics in the true sense of the word; these are books children want to read again and again. Adults can recall them fondly from their own childhoods and enjoy them again with their own children. These talking-animals stories seem so real; no wonder my students create projects where Wilbur, Stuart, and Louis, meet each other in story after story. Studying White and his writing makes an impression on my young writers that they are not likely to forget.

There are other wonderful writers of classic children's books that may well lend themselves to similar author studies. Beatrix Potter would be lovely for younger children. Laura Ingalls Wilder's works are still much beloved, if controversial for their problematic negative depiction of Native Americans. However, a deep look at her works might be just the way for students to dig deep into the attitudes of the time along with providing what she does not provide: the Native American viewpoint. A. A. Milne is another writer who may be as familiar and comforting as White is to many. However, more recent authors are great too. William Steig is a wonderful choice for an author study for readers of all ages

Stuart and Wilbur

by Michael Benhabib

My name is Stuart Little. A few years ago I wrote a book about part of my life called *Stuart Little*, but I never finished it. I just published it and forgot about it. This was a big mistake because there's so much more to tell. So I decided to write the sequel to *Stuart Little*, *Stuart and Wilbur*.

It must have been about 2 or 3 hours after I drove out of Ames' Crossing when I came across a sign that read "Zuckerman's Famous Pig." There was an arrow pointing in the direction of a small dirt road. I was curious so I followed the arrow. The road was bumpy and there were trees on either side of it. This looked like the exact place I might find Margalo in. Margalo was my best friend. She was a red bird that disappeared from my parents' house in New York City. That was when I started my journey north to look for Margalo.

When I got to the end of the road I looked to the right of me and there was a house. Just a plain simple wooden house. To the left of me there was a barn. The barn was red and it wasn't very big and from the end of the road I could hear noises. All different kinds of noises. The noises of animals.

So I started to move closer and closer towards the barn until I was right next to the barn door. The door was open so I was just able to drive in. In the barn I saw all different kinds of animals: a pig, three spiders, a goose and some goslings, a lamb and there was a rat eating from the pig's trough. The animals in the barn stopped what they were doing and stared at me. The pig walked up to my car and said, "Hello, my name is Wilbur. Welcome to Zuckerman's barn."

"Hi, my name is Stuart Little. Have you seen a red bird lately?"

"No," said one of the spiders. "Why do you ask?" I told all the animals all about Margalo and why I was there.

Then one of the spiders said, "That's very sad."

"Yes, I know," I said. "By the way," I continued, "What is your name, please?"

"My name is Joy," said the spider. "And that's Aranea."

"I'm Nellie," said another one of the spiders.

(Stuart decides to stay at the barn in Templeton's nest.)

After a while I got very used to the barn and I thought I'd never leave. Actually, the barn was very nice, although Templeton seemed to have problems living with someone.

One afternoon I was talking to Wilbur about how much I liked this barn when I heard the sound of birds singing. I went outside and to my surprise I saw Margalo sitting on a tree and singing. I opened my

mouth to speak but no words came out. Margalo
stopped singing and flew down to me. Once Margalo
had reached the ground she stammered, "S-S-S-Stuart?
Is that you?"

"Y-Y-Yes," I stuttered.

"What are you doing here? How did you get here?"
she said.

"Well," I answered, "I came looking for you."

(Margalo tells Stuart all her adventures and decides
to move into Templeton's nest with Stuart.)

"SHE'S NOT STAYING IN MY NEST!" Templeton said
in a loud voice.

"Oh, please let her stay!" begged Wilbur.

"Definitely not!" said Templeton.

"Oh, Templeton, you are nothing but a selfish rat!"
said Wilbur in a loud voice.

"Fine, if you insist," said Templeton.

So Margalo stayed in Templeton's nest for many
days. After a while she got very used to the barn and
thought that she would never leave.

The barn was a very peaceful place. Year after year
Margalo and I lived there and we are living there still.

Charlotte's Web: The Next Chapter

by Nathaniel Shapiro

Note to Reader:

You might be wondering what happened after Charlotte's Web. It tells you only a bit about what happened. So without further ado I will present to you what happened to some characters.

Fern—Fern was very proud of her award winning pig. Throughout the many years in schools she had really good grades, and she was able to go to college. At age 27 she married Henry Fussy. Now they live in a nice suburban home with their dog and three children. She is now writing a book called "How Animals Act."

Avery—Unlike his sister Avery did not get the best grades in school. Since he always liked to play with toy guns, he was interested in the Army. At age 18 he went into the Army. Currently he is a well respected major running a base in Arkansas. He is very happy with his life and is currently engaged.

The Goose and the Gander—The goose and the gander lived a long life. Fortunately the Zuckermans don't have a taste for goose but they do for goose eggs. Every year the geese lay eggs that the Zuckermans eat and sell. They are considered to be the best eggs in the country. Year after year the geese and the ganders born from this family still say everything three times.

No matter how the animals try, no one can break that pattern of speech.

Templeton—As for the rat he lived a long and healthy life. Even though Lurvy never stopped chasing him, he never found where the rat claimed residence. Every year after that when Wilbur went to the fair Templeton followed. One year Templeton met a beautiful young rat at the fair and they married. They now have 6 children and Templeton has become the new coach for Wilbur by finding him new words for Charlotte's descendents to write on the web. Templeton and Wilbur now have long discussions about the way things are at the farm.

Charlotte's Family—Year after year thousands of little tiny spiders get born into Charlotte's family. Now her offspring is spreading all over the world and teaching pigs and also saving their lives.

Wilbur—Wilbur still acts very humble, but is some pig considering he is world famous. Every fall to the spring he watches the eggs of Charlotte's descendants as carefully as he did the first time. Every year he goes to the fair and wins first prize. No one has ever beat him, and he recently found out that uncle the pig is his uncle. Now they live together on Zuckerman's farm peacefully. Wilbur finally knows that Zuckerman will never even think of having him for ham or bacon.

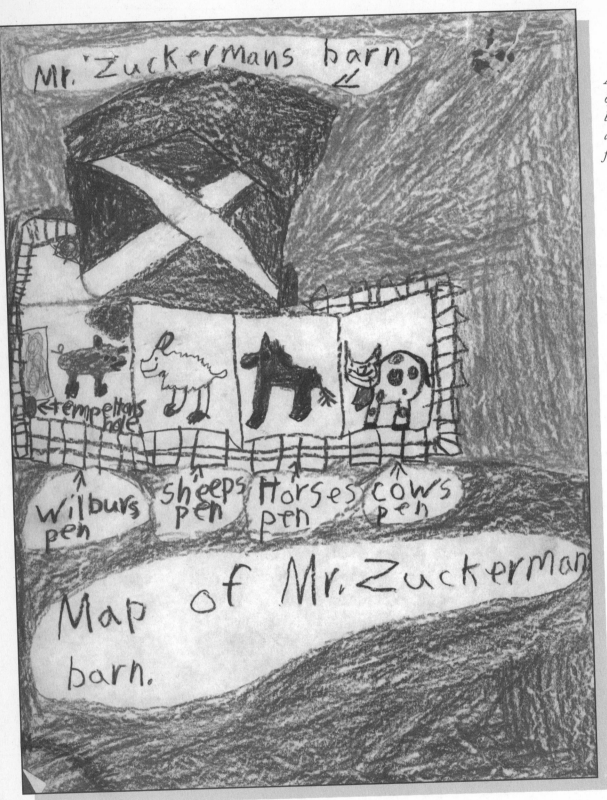

Mr. Zuckermans barn

etempeltons hole

Wilburs pen   Sheeps pen   Horses pen   Cows pen

Map of Mr. Zuckerman barn.

A student's map of Zuckerman's barn, prepared as part of the final project

STUDENT PACKET

E. B. WHITE: An Author Study

INTRODUCTION

Charlotte's Web, Stuart Little, and *The Trumpet of the Swan* are three of the most well-known and best-loved books ever written for children. No doubt many of you are familiar with some or all of these books. You may have had *Stuart Little* read to you when you were little and watched the movie of *Charlotte's Web* more than once. Or you may have read all three books on your own. Those of you new to these books are in for a treat—they are truly wonderful stories.

For this first literature study we will be looking at the work of E. B. White. Not only will we read and discuss his children's books, but we will learn about White himself, his approach to writing, and how others have responded to his work.

BIOGRAPHICAL BACKGROUND

Elwyn Brooks White was born on July 11, 1899, in Mount Vernon, a suburb of New York City. His father was a piano manufacturer. His mother was very musical and also loved nature, traits she passed on to her son. White was an early avid reader and quickly became an accomplished writer, sending stories and poems to *St. Nicholas Magazine*, a popular journal for children. A great lover of outdoor activities, White suffered from terrible hay fever, so his family decided to spend their summers in Maine where his hay fever wasn't so bad. White loved these summers and his fond memories show up in his writing, especially in *Stuart Little* and *The Trumpet of the Swan*.

White went to Cornell University and upon graduation began a career in journalism. After working at several newspapers and traveling throughout America, he moved to New York City and began writing for *The New Yorker*, then a new weekly magazine. Before long he took an editing job at the magazine and stayed associated with the magazine for the rest of his life. In 1929 he married Katherine Angell, a fellow editor at *The New Yorker*. Their son, Joel, was born a year later. Beginning in 1931, the Whites summered in Maine, eventually buying a farm and moving there in 1938. Six years later they moved back to New York, continuing to spend summers in Maine. Finally, in 1957, they moved back to Maine full-time. Whether in New York or Maine, White wrote. He was a great letter writer as well as a poet, essayist, and reporter. He died on October 1, 1985.

CHARLOTTE'S WEB

E. B. White spent a long time writing *Charlotte's Web*. He began work on a first draft in 1950, completing it on January 19, 1951. After numerous revisions the book was published to great acclaim on October 15, 1952. White did a tremendous amount of research for *Charlotte's Web*, watching life on the farm and learning all he could about spiders.

MEMORIES OF CHARLOTTE'S WEB

What do you know of *Charlotte's Web*? Was it read to you or do you know it in some other way? Please write your personal experiences with the story here. We will discuss these experiences with the whole class.

_____

_____

_____

_____

_____

_____

_____

_____

READING
CHARLOTTE'S WEB

To begin, we will all read *Charlotte's Web.* Each of you will have your own copy of the book. This way you can make the book your own. As we study the book, you may find parts that are special to you. Underline them, note them, write in the book and make it your personal *Charlotte's Web.* E. B. White wrote his *Charlotte's Web,* but we all bring our own experiences to a reading of the book. Someone who has lived on a farm will read the book differently from someone who has only lived in a city. This means that my *Charlotte's Web* will be different from yours.

Remember, everyone in this class is part of our reading community. This means that we will decide together how much time *everyone* in the class needs to comfortably read the book. Fast readers are not necessarily good readers. In a community of readers, everyone is respected as a reader. Those who take their time reading a book are as important in our reading community as those who will finish a book in a day. If you finish *Charlotte's Web* before others, you should continue reading your independent book. Realize that even if you have read this book 10 times already, you will need to read it again for this assignment. Scholars reread books many times to better understand them. I reread *Charlotte's Web* every year, and learn something more about it every time I read it. If you reread it with the idea that you are reading it in a new way and hoping to learn something new, it will be an enjoyable experience for you. That is what being a literary scholar is all about.

READING PLAN FOR *CHARLOTTE'S WEB*

Work out a schedule for completing the book by the agreed-upon date.

Week   Chapters

_____

_____

_____

_____

_____

Due date: _____

RESPONDING TO *CHARLOTTE'S WEB*

We will not discuss *Charlotte's Web* as a whole class until everyone has finished reading it. However, you are welcome to discuss it with your classmates, with me, and with your family. If you are bursting to talk about an event in the book, please do so! Just do so quietly so that others can read. If you are at home, by all means read a favorite section aloud to your little sister or brother, or even to your mother! Use your journals for written responses. I love to read your entries and write back to you.

STUDYING
CHARLOTTE'S WEB

Once everyone has finished the book we will discuss it as a whole class. First we will just discuss what we enjoyed about the book, what we noticed, what struck us most. Then we will look more closely at the book as literary scholars. I will present some of the methods scholars use when studying an author and particular books. Specifically, you will learn how to annotate your copy of *Charlotte's Web*. This means underlining lines in the book that seem important to you and writing notes about the book in the margins. We will do a close reading of the first chapter all together and then each of you will do a close study of one chapter and present your findings to the class.

During our work with *Charlotte's Web*, we will listen to a tape of White reading *Charlotte's Web* and learn more about him as a writer. As we learn about the way he wrote *Charlotte's Web*, we will be learning more about what it means to be a writer.

CHAPTER STUDY

You are to do a "close reading" of one chapter of *Charlotte's Web*. Don't feel every page or every paragraph will have something to note. Each chapter is different and each of you will respond differently.

Here are some suggestions of what to look for:

❀ <u>Life and death words.</u> Remember how Fern translated her father's "do away with it" to "kill it." See what words you can discover in your chapter.

❀ <u>Irony</u>. This is the way an author makes fun of something by writing the opposite of what he really means. An example of irony is in Chapter 1 when Mr. Arable says to Avery that "I only distribute pigs to early risers." In fact, Mr. Arable lets Fern keep the pig because she was so passionate, not because she was up early.

* <u>Foreshadowing</u>. This is when something in the book hints at something that will happen later in the book. In Chapter 1 bacon is mentioned as part of the Arables' breakfast — and, of course, that is what Wilbur is to become!

* <u>Lists.</u> E. B. White loves to use lists of stuff in his descriptions. See if you can find some in your chapter.

* <u>Smells, tastes, looks, and more.</u> E. B. White writes amazing description. Not just what things look like, but what they smell, sound, and feel like. Be sure to note the wonderful descriptions that are in your chapter.

* <u>Friendship.</u> This is a big theme in the book. See what references you can find in your chapter that are about friendship.

* <u>Comparisons.</u> There are many. Some are between animals and people, others between children and adults, and others may still need to be discovered. See if you can be the first person to find a new comparison in your chapter!

* <u>Writing</u>. There are many, many references to writing in this book. See if you can find the less obvious ones (such as the words on the web).

* <u>Changes</u>. Another theme of the book. Characters change. Seasons change. See if there are indications of change in your chapter.

* <u>Anything else you think is interesting.</u> Surprise us!

Use the chart on the next page to record your notes and observations. Remember to include the page number and write the quote.

Notes for *Charlotte's Web*

Chapter # _____ Chapter Title _____

Page	Quote	Note

QUESTIONS TO PONDER AND DISCUSS ABOUT *CHARLOTTE'S WEB*

Every year many questions come up during our discussions. The two that follow are great for getting started. Please answer them thoughtfully in preparation for our class discussion.

Who do you think is the hero? Why?

_____

_____

_____

_____

_____

_____

Who do you think is selfish? Why?

_____

_____

_____

_____

_____

_____

_____

_____

STUART LITTLE

White's first children's book was *Stuart Little.* He had been telling Stuart stories to nieces, nephews, and his son for years before he decided to write them down. He began writing the book in 1939 and then put it away until 1944, when he finished it. *Stuart Little* came out in October 1945. It was a huge success, eventually translated into 20 languages.

THE TRUMPET OF THE SWAN

The Trumpet of the Swan was White's last children's book. He used memories of his childhood camp in Maine as well as the careful research he always did for his books. His manuscript for the book was completed in 1969, and White sent it right to his editor rather than putting it away for a while as he had done with his other books. An immediate success like his other children's books, *The Trumpet of the Swan* quickly became a best-seller. Today, it is less known than *Charlotte's Web* and *Stuart Little,* but it is still widely read.

STUART LITTLE AND THE TRUMPET OF THE SWAN STUDY GROUPS

You will select either *Stuart Little* or *The Trumpet of the Swan* for this part of the unit and read, discuss, and study it with others in the class who are reading the same book. You are welcome to read all three books, but I would like you to spend some time in a smaller group studying one book in depth. Finally, the whole class will come together for a discussion on all of the books, how they connect, and some final thoughts on White and his books.

What connections can you see between *Charlotte's Web* and the book you read (*Stuart Little/The Trumpet of the Swan*)?

_____

_____

_____

_____

_____

_____

_____

_____

_____

FINAL E. B. WHITE PROJECTS

As a final response to this unit, you will create a project that will combine all you have felt and learned from reading and studying White's children's books.

Here are some ideas, but you are welcome to come up with your own:

- ❀ Create a piece of art combining characters and scenes from the different books.

- ❀ Create a map of one of the books.

- ❀ Create an original comic book using characters from the different books.

- ❀ Create a skit or play using characters and ideas from the books.

- ❀ Create a story about E. B. White and characters from his books.

- ❀ Write a sequel to one of the books.

Using Beloved Classics to Deepen Reading Comprehension • Scholastic Professional Books

- ❀ Create a puppet show with characters from the books.
- ❀ Write an original story inspired by the books.
- ❀ Create a video about the books.
- ❀ Create a poem inspired by the books.
- ❀ Come up with your own idea.

PROJECT PLAN

Please write a description of your project and a plan for completing it in a timely fashion.

_____

_____

_____

_____

_____

_____

_____

_____

_____

_____

_____

_____

_____

_____

Project due: _____

Digging Deep into Theme: A Study *of* Cinderella

"It's like being Cinderella. You wear your suit and go there and you have to be back in the projects by midnight."

—JAMEL OESER-SWEAT, WESTINGHOUSE SCIENCE
TALENT SEARCH FINALIST
NEW YORK TIMES, JANUARY 30, 1994

Fairy tales are fantasy stories that everyone knows. References to fairy tales abound in our lives. We use them without thinking: "What a witch!" "If the shoe fits." "The wolf is at the door." A thematic study of one well-known fairy tale can provide children with a deeper understanding of traditional literature as well as an opportunity to explore the myriad ways the tale has become part of our culture. *Cinderella* is particularly suitable for such a study because it seems so universal. The theme we associate with *Cinderella* is "rags to riches," a compelling one that manifests itself over and over again in tales, literature, and images all over the world. It is recognizable in the ad for a new, improved detergent that makes clothes clean (ashes to ball gown) as well as in the poor boy who becomes a great president (Abraham Lincoln). The study can go in numerous directions depending on the interest of the teacher and students. Opportunities exist for exploring the tale in other cultures, in parodies, in comparison to other tales, in popular culture, in history, and in literature. It is a unit rich with possibilities.

DIGGING DEEP INTO THEME

great way to get children digging deep into literature is through a thematic study. Thematic studies can be grounded in content from many disciplines. For example, my fall social studies unit is on immigration. I use a wide variety of materials during this study including an abundance of literature. We dig deep into works of historical fiction, biography, memoir, and other genres to see what we can learn about the immigrant experience from a variety of viewpoints. A teacher friend builds a thematic study around one book, Jean Craighead George's *Julie of the Wolves*. In addition to digging deep into the book itself, my friend's students research wolves, the arctic, and more. They end up knowing a tremendous amount of the content on which the novel is based as well as a great deal about the work itself.

Folklore lends itself well to thematic studies because you can take it in so many different directions. While I focus on the specific tale of *Cinderella*, it is also possible to focus more generally on one genre, for example: fairy tales, fables, or myths. Alternatively, a class could focus on the folklore of a particular culture, say the Anansi stories of West Africa. Or they could compare and contrast myths across several cultures.

Whatever the content and approach, such thematic studies are terrific vehicles to get children digging deep into literature.

CINDERELLA BACKGROUND

SOME HISTORY

Versions of the *Cinderella* story have been around in one form or another for hundreds of years. The ninth-century Chinese manuscript of *Yeh Shen* is thought to be the oldest written version of the tale. Charles Perrault popularized the tale in Europe by including it in his 1697 fairy tale collection, *Tales of My Mother Goose*. It is the Perrault version, complete with fairy godmother, pumpkin, and glass slippers, that has become the definitive *Cinderella* for Americans today, mostly due to Disney's 1949 animated film. However, less well-known versions exist from many different parts of the world. The German Grimm Brothers published their version (sans godmother) in their 19-century collection of fairy tales. While the version we know seems distinctly European, folklorists are constantly discovering non-Western variants of the tale. Modern writers have also taken to the tale, often parodying it or utilizing the rags-to-riches theme for their own purposes.

CINDERELLA TALE TYPES

Folklorists use the term "tale type" to refer to a particular story line. Marian Roalfe Cox noted five types in *Cinderella, Three Hundred and Forty-Five Variants of Cinderella, Catskin, and Cap o'Rushes, Abstracted and Tabulated*

(1893). Aarne and Thompson identified three types in *The Types of the Folktale* (1961). Both note significant elements such as the persecuted heroine, magical help, the ball, and the slipper test. Neil Philip, in *The Cinderella Story* (1988), writes "There are numerous ways of categorizing the Cinderella variants, depending on the nature and the order of the incidents. Many areas have distinctive traditions. But it is essentially true to say that there are two main strands of story: one in which the girl is mistreated and humiliated because of her stepmother's jealousy, and one in which her suffering is caused by her father's incestuous desires" (p. 3). Teachers seriously committed to this unit need to be aware of both strands since the former is the only one that tends to be found in children's books, though there are occasionally veiled allusions to the latter. Perrault's *Cinderella* typifies the former strand while Charlotte Huck's *Princess Furball* (1989) is a sanitized version of the latter.

CINDERELLA IN THE CLASSROOM

THE CINDERELLA CENTER

I have a classroom divided into work areas, meeting areas, and a cozy reading area, carpeted and full of pillows with a classroom library located nearby. For each new literary study I set up a learning center in my reading area. Sometimes there are only a few books and students add their own work to the center as the unit gets underway. In the case of the *Cinderella* study, I create a full-fledged learning center, designed to excite and intrigue my students. Picture books and fairy tale collections are invitingly displayed as well as cartoons, ads, newspaper headlines, and other *Cinderella* references. It is easy to build a collection for this unit. Publishers are constantly coming out with inexpensive new versions of this old tale as well as fairy tale collections. School and public libraries are generally well stocked with fairy tales. You will be amazed how often you will see references to *Cinderella* once you begin such a unit. Keep an eye out for references in advertisements and in magazine and newspaper headlines.

Encourage your students to add to the center. As we got deeper into our study and our definition of what a *Cinderella* tale is broadened, my students relished the search for the nonconventional *Cinderella*— Charles Dickens's *Oliver Twist* or a tale of a baseball rookie who made it big. Parents and others in the school community should also be encouraged to contribute.

GETTING STARTED

I begin the *Cinderella* study by reading a silly *Cinderella* variant such as Roald Dahl's in *Revolting Rhymes* (1998) or Babette Cole's *Prince Cinders* (1987) to whet my students' appetites for the fun ahead. I then give each child a packet which includes an introduction to the unit, activities, charts, and a bibliography (see page 69).

PERSONAL FAIRY TALE DEFINITIONS

The first activity in the packet asks students to write their own definitions of the term *fairy tale*. I encourage them to write whatever they wish. I assure them that there is no such thing as one "right" definition for *fairy tale*. My students' initial definitions have included fairy tales as "fantasy or illusion," full of "dragons and wizards," and "a fiction book that is the kind of book that a mother can read to her four-year-old son or daughter."

Here is a chart of one class's definitions of *fairy tale* at the beginning of the unit and, in parentheses, their comments after weeks of study.

A FAIRY TALE IS:

- based on a long time ago (but doesn't have to be)

- a story that takes place in a faraway land that doesn't exist (sometimes, but doesn't have to)

- normally concentrated on one person (yes)

- a story where they live "happily ever after" (yes)

- made-up, fake, not real, or fiction (yes)

- something usually with a moral (yes)

- usually with someone wishing (not always)

- a story with a fairy (not always)

- something with magic in it (yes)

- something with a bad person in it (mostly yes; the person can also be irritating, mean, and/or jealous)

- something with many versions (yes)

- a story that begins with "Once upon a time" (or something similar)

- usually a children's book (no)

- something that wouldn't happen here today (maybe?)

- full of expressions of happiness and sadness (yes)

- something that includes things like witches (more often than not)

- something you can read but goes up in your mind (yes)

MEMORIES OF *CINDERELLA*

Next I have the students retell *Cinderella*. For this activity we sit in a circle. Students either volunteer to add to the evolving story, or I simply have them tell parts of the story as we go around the circle. Of course, it quickly becomes clear where their memories of *Cinderella* come from—the Disney movie, of course! Sometimes, they will have vague recollections of someone reading the story to them, but for the vast majority it is Disney's version (especially those mice) that stays in their memories!

ANALYSES OF SOME *CINDERELLA* VARIANTS

We now move into the heart of the unit. Students are asked to investigate a wide variety of *Cinderella* variants and keep track of their research in charts provided as part of their packets. The charts are structured to encourage students to expand their idea of what a *Cinderella* story is. The information is intentionally kept to a minimum so that filling out the charts isn't a chore or simply a mindless task. Students quickly learn what a genre is and enjoy distinguishing picture books from videos from poems and chapter books in their explorations. I have found that the setting category occasionally gives them trouble. There is no problem with obvious variants like Shirley Climo's *The Korean Cinderella* (1989). Difficulties come up with more subtle distinctions like American versus Canadian or American versions of Perrault's French story. However, such dilemmas also reinforce the idea that fairy tales can't be simplified and labeled in any one way. Finally, the personal response section gives students a quick and easy way to give their own opinions about the versions they are studying. I ask for deeper, more insightful responses in their journals.

Students explore *Cinderella* variants in many ways: individual or paired readings, read-alouds, and videos. To begin their explorations of *Cinderella,* I require that everyone in the class be exposed to a number of variants, which give us all a frame of reference for discussion. Some of these required texts are read by students independently or in pairs; others I read aloud to the class. Students then move on to choose from among the many texts available to them.

I set aside a *Cinderella* time every day. It is structured to be quite predictable: I begin with a group experience, perhaps reading a *Cinderella* to the whole group or leading a discussion on a text all have read. At this time I allow discussion of other media versions of *Cinderella*—for example, a television show or ad. After the whole-group time there is some workshop time which the children use to read alone or with a friend and to work on filling in their charts.

TEXTS

RECOMMENDED STUDENT READINGS

Perrault, Charles. (1969). "Cinderella or The Little Glass Slipper." Trns. A. E. Johnson. In *Perrault's Fairy Tales.* New York: Dover.

This is an early English translation of Perrault's tale. I feel it is very important for students to read the original Perrault since it is the one the Disney film is based on and so the one they are most likely to know. This particular version is easy for students to read. Many other early editions have small type and archaic conventions (such as no quotation marks in dialogues) which make them challenging for young readers. The Dover edi-

tion's print is large and the style is familiar. I ask my students to read this text on their own. Some read it aloud with partners, others silently alone. Since they are already familiar with the plot, the vocabulary does not seem to be a problem for them. They seemed comfortable using context clues to help them with unfamiliar words. However, for students who do find the vocabulary a challenge, I recommend creating a glossary to help them with the reading.

Brothers Grimm. (1987). "Cinderella." In *The Complete Fairy Tales of the Brothers Grimm.* Trns. by Jack Zipes. New York: Bantam.

After Perrault, the Grimm fairy tales are most well known to us. However, we tend to be less familiar with the Grimm version of *Cinderella.* My students are invariably surprised by the lack of a godmother and the harshness of certain elements of the text, such as the cutting off of the stepsisters' toe and heel and the pecking out of their eyes at the end. Certainly adults have been uncomfortable with this imagery in the past, with the result that the Perrault version, which has no blood, has dominated. Much has been written about the Grimm tales and their effect on children. Today, with all the violence of video games, television shows, and films such as *Home Alone,* the Grimm tales seem mild.

There are many versions of the Grimm tales available. This one is well translated and my students have had no difficulty reading it independently despite its small print.

Chase, Richard. (1976). "Ashpet." In *Grandfather Tales,* Boston: Houghton Mifflin.

My students read this Appalachian variant on their own. It is clearly based on the well-known European versions, yet the landscape and language are those of the American Appalachian people. It would also work well as a read-aloud or even in a storytelling situation. Later in the unit students are able to contrast this version with Tom Davenport's film, a very different *Ashpet,* as well as a picture-book version retold by Joanne Compton. It is interesting to contrast all three. There are also a number of picture books of this tale. It can be fun to compare Chase's retelling with both the Davenport film and the picture books.

Steptoe, John. (1987). *Mufaro's Beautiful Daughters.* New York: Lothrop, Lee & Shepard Books.

    This is a beautiful book. Students can savor it on their own, in pairs, or in a group reading using the big book version. Steptoe was inspired by a visit to Zimbabwe and a story he found in a 19th century collection of South African folktales. It is a different telling of the *Cinderella* story in a totally different environment and provides an excellent transition into versions that don't have balls, pumpkins, and shoe tests. However, it is not exactly an African folktale. For this reason, I do not recommend using it to teach about African culture, but rather as Steptoe's own *Cinderella* based on his visit to Zimbabwe.

Louie, Ai-Ling. (1982). *Yeh-Shen.* Illustrated by Ed Young. New York: Philomel.
Wilson, Barbara Ker. (1993). *Wishbones.* Illustrated by Meilo So. New York: Bradbury.

    These are two very beautiful, non-Western tellings of the oldest *Cinderella* story. The Louie book has a copy of the Chinese text in the front. Before I had the Wilson book I used only Louie's book. During one of my class discussions of the tale a Chinese teacher was visiting. She told us that Louie had not completed the tale, ending it with the marriage when it actually went on beyond that. Wilson's book continues the story to its ancient conclusion. It is interesting that Louie chose to end the story prematurely at the point where Westerns are most comfortable, while Wilson was more true to the original text. This makes for an interesting discussion. Additionally, our Chinese visitor was fascinated that we would even consider Yeh-Shen a *Cinderella.* She told us the Chinese consider *Cinderella* to be the European tale alone.

TEACHER READ-ALOUDS

Viorst, Judith. (1987). "...And Then the Prince Knelt Down and Tried to Put the Glass Slipper on Cinderella's Foot." In *Don't Bet on The Prince: Contemporary Feminist Fairy Tales in North America and England* New York: Routledge.

    This is an extremely brief, witty poem. I read it aloud at the beginning of our study.

Dahl, Roald. "Cinderella." (1988). In *Revolting Rhymes.* Illustrated by Quentin Blake. New York: Bantam.

    The book's title says it all. Dahl relishes turning everything in the tale around in a singsong verse. I use this early on to illustrate how well-known authors parody the tale.

Cole, Babette. (1987). *Prince Cinders.* New York: Sandcastle Books.

    Here we have a gender switch done with wit and humor. It is a good way to introduce the idea that Cinderella does not have to be a girl. I have recently discovered a charming video version that students enjoy as well.

Perlman, Janet. (1992). *Cinderella Penguin or The Little Glass Flipper.* Toronto: We Can Press.

This is a highly visual parody. In addition to being amused by the very concept of roly-poly penguins as princess, students enjoy seeking out small jokes in the illustrations. For example, on the walls of Cinderella's home are several penguin-enhanced well-known pieces of art. Thus, the famous Unicorn Tapestry is now a penguin-unicorn.

Edwards, Pamela Duncan. (1997). *Dinorella.* Illustrated by Henry Cole. New York: Hyperion.

This is great fun to read aloud. The alliterative language is very clever and my students enjoy it tremendously. Couple the witty text with equally amusing illustrations and you have a most engaging read-aloud.

Yorink, Arthur. (1990). *Ugh.* Illustrated by Richard Egielski. New York: Farrar Straus Giroux.

I admit to tremendous fondness for this picture book. It is another male Cinderella situated in an ersatz Stone Age. The plot line, text, and illustrations are very clever, especially the twist on the slipper test.

Lardner, Ring. (1926). "Cinderella." In *What Of It?* New York: Scribner's.

This is a delightful 1920s parody of the classic tale. Lardner has a free hand with the vernacular and activities of the period (think *Guys and Dolls*). Cinderella is Zelda and the Prince is named Scott (Fitzgerald, perhaps?). I am selective about which classes I read this to. They need to have sufficient context to get the humor. Otherwise they are just puzzled.

Sexton, Anne. (1971). "Cinderella." In *Transformations.* Boston: Houghton Mifflin.

I read this aloud to my class. It is an adult poem, but the feeling of disappointment is something that students can understand. In the real world, fairy tales don't always happen. This poem is a sardonic looking back by a Cinderella who found it wasn't quite "happily ever after."

Levine, Gail Carson. (1997). *Ella Enchanted.* New York: HarperTrophy.

The Newbery Honor novel *Ella Enchanted* is a different sort of read-aloud. I had a wonderful time reading this to my class the year it was published. We were already several weeks into our *Cinderella* study when I started it as our end-of-day novel read-aloud. I told them that I was reading it aloud for a reason; that it connected to something we were studying. I further told the children to come and whisper in my ear if they figured out what it was. The children quickly figured out that it was a fairy tale. However, the *Cinderella*-connection took some time. Levine is very subtle in her use of the *Cinderella* tale. Ella is so feisty that she seems completely unlike the more typically docile Cinderellas of Disney and Perrault. However, before long my students caught on and by the end they were cheering Ella on.

VIDEO *CINDERELLAS*

There are movies galore about *Cinderella.* The rags-to-riches theme is remarkably prevalent in Hollywood movies. Every year there seem to be a few out, often related to sports. My students adore exploring this theme in film. I usually show all or parts of several films and then lead discussions contrasting and comparing the films to each other as well as to printed materials. In the bibliography are a number of *Cinderella* and *Cinderella*-themed movies. I have found the following videos to work with great success:

Rossini's La Cenerentola.

This is a version filmed at La Scala in Milan. Evidently there was already a *Cinderella* opera out at the time that Rossini began this one, so there is no shoe test; rather, bracelets are featured. I like exposing my students to a different medium such as opera, and this particular version is so well done that they quite enjoy the parts I show.

Jerry Lewis's Cinderfella.

Students love this one! It takes place in 1960's Beverly Hills with Ed Wynn as a rather rotund fairy godfather. A patent leather evening shoe is featured during the ball.

Tom Davenport's Ashpet.

This is a delightful version of the Appalachian story, different from Chase's version. An African-American storyteller is Aunt Sally, the fairy godmother of this version.

Usually when I'm leading a discussion comparing versions I like to make a chart. I made the chart on the following page as we compared the three videos. The students chose the categories.

THE *CINDERELLA* THEME IN POPULAR CULTURE AND ELSEWHERE

 encourage my students to look beyond the usual places to find the rags-to-riches theme. Many enjoy looking on the sports pages. For example,

the stunning upset of the semifinals for the 1994 World Cup involved underdog Bulgaria defeating the expected winner Germany. The *New York Times* headline of July 11, 1994, was: "Bulgaria, a Small Foot in Soccer, Steps Closer to Glass Slipper." Another child was able to convince me that Disney's *Aladdin* was a Cinderella story, very much a rags-to-riches tale. Chapter books such as Burnett's *The Little Princess* are often mentioned.

STUDENT RESPONSES TO *CINDERELLAS*

esponse journals are part of the fabric of my classroom. Thus, my students are comfortable when asked to write a more extended response to a particular video or books. Here's a sampling of responses to some Cinderella variants:

Lexy's response to *Cinderfella*:

I thought it was very funny and nice. It was very different than most Cinderellas. For instance in this one Fella was pretty dumb and not too handsome. But Cinderella is always very pretty.

I liked the fairy godfather. He was really funny. Especially with his wise cracks. I think Charlie Chaplin would make a good Fella because Chaplin is just perfect for the role.

My response to Lexy:

Dear Lexy,

I am intrigued by your idea of Chaplin as Fella. Actually, don't you think some of his films are *Cinderella* stories? (I'd shown a number of Chaplin shorts and features to my class.) His Little Tramp character is

COMPARING VIDEO CINDIES

Categories	*La Cenerentola*	*Cinderfella*	Ashpet
Family	mean stepfather silly stepsisters: mean and greedy	stepmother and stepbrothers mean, just want money. (stepmother feels sorry at end)	stepmother: nice stepsisters: mean
Magical helper	Aliadoro prince's tutor	fairy godfather	Aunt Sally
Where they lived	house in countryside	LA mansion	farmhouse
Ball	Ball	Ball	Goodbye dance for soldiers
Test object	bracelets	patent leather dress shoe	glass shoe
Test	Valet/Prince Switch (Cinderella falls for valet who is really the prince)	People/Person (Jerry is People, Princess is Person)	Niceness Riddles True Love
Culture	Italian	Californian	Appalachian
Time	1800s	1960s	World War II
Animals	none	fish	horse

certainly a Cinderella-like person, don't you think? Check out *Modern Times*—see if that is a *Cinderella* story.

Eric on his favorite variant:

I liked the Grimm Brothers *Cinderella* because sometimes I think that other *Cinderellas* are too babyish (At least at my age that's what I think.) For example, when the birds poke the stepsisters' eyes out. I don't think any mom would tell their 3 year old son that.

Eric on the *Cinderella* theme in an independent reading book:

I am reading a book called *Charlie and the Chocolate Factory*. It is very good. I like it because Charlie (a boy who loves chocolate), who lives in a very poor family, all of a sudden becomes the owner of Mr. Wonka's giant chocolate factory. I think it is kind of a *Cinderella* story. The "ball" is the tour of the chocolate factory. Then when Charlie becomes the owner of the chocolate factory, that is kind of like Cinderella with the prince except the "palace" is the chocolate factory.

COMPARING *CINDERELLA* TO ANOTHER FAIRY TALE

After my students have spent some time on *Cinderella,* I ask them to select another fairy tale as a comparison. Then they become storytellers, practicing the tale and telling it to their classmates just as the tales were originally told. I then ask them to write how their favorite *Cinderella* variant is similar to and different from this tale.

LETTERS TO CINDERELLA

Recently I added a new twist to our *Cinderella* studies, a letter to one of the many literary Cindies in our classroom collection. For a change of pace, I suggest that students, who are used to writing letters to me in their journals, write to Cinderella as well. I began this activity last year by reading *Prince Cinders* aloud. Afterwards I modeled how I would write a letter to the central character (see sample below). I thought aloud, revised on the chart, and did the best I could to make my writing process as transparent as possible. Each student then selected one *Cinderella,* read it, and then composed a letter to the main character. After revising and proof-reading it, each wrote it on a nice piece of stationery.

My model "Dear Cindy" letter

Dear Prince Cinders,

I've gotten to know a number of fairy tale characters, but you are one of the most unusual. Most Cinderella-types I've come across want beauty — you wanted to be big and hairy like your brothers. Weird! Perrault's Cinderella sure didn't seem to want to be anything like her step-sisters.

How lucky that Princess Lovelypenny thought you saved her from your-self. Now that you are married have you told her the truth?

Since you wanted to be so big I hope the palace has a good gym. And I hope your brothers keep things clean.

Lastly, what happened to those trousers? Did you put them in a royal museum or throw them out?

I look forward to hearing from you.

Most respectfully,

Monica Edinger

Dear Cinderella,

I think you should have started a rebellion. But then you probably wouldn't have gone to the ball in nice clothes because your reputation would have been ruined and then you wouldn't have married the prince. By the way only the stupidest man on earth would have married your sisters. Also, does that fairy godmother have a magic license? She was very surprised when her spells worked. Well, you and the prince are a cool duo.

Sincerely,
Nicolai

Dear Yeh-Shen,

I very much admire your beliefs. I suppose you remind me of me. I have always wanted to go to China. If I picked one place in the world to go, it would be China, by far. Please tell me a little about your homeland.

I am very sorry about your fish. I bet everyone is still praying to your fish and maybe something wonderful will happen! If I was a girl I would always want to dress like you. But unfortunately I am male. I hope your stepsisters will be dissed and miss your mother greatly. She was a great woman in my understanding. If my mother died I would be in the same sadness.

You have the largest heart in the land. You own the greatest slippers in the land. What did you end up doing with the slipper? You are so fortunate that the slipper fit the foot. It must have been like golden honey. Did you know the slipper was going to fit on your foot? Please tell me your emotions at this time. Just in case this ever happen to me. This was a bit and fast change in your life. One minute you are being treated badly by your stepmother. The next minute you are a princess. It must feel great. Hey, you are free. Life can't get much better than that.

Tell me about the palace. Tell me all the secrets. What do people call you? What should I call you? I hope you have the best with the prince in the palace. I am eager to get your response. This is exciting. Thank you so much!

Yours truly,
Zachary

REDEFINING FAIRY TALE

fter several weeks of research, discussion, and analysis, I ask my students to consider their definition of *fairy tale* and to write a new definition based on their work. We have a class discussion about these definitions, whether they have changed, and if so why. Then we attempt to create a class definition of fairy tales. The following chart was created during one such discussion. It is full of phrases taken from students, by no means a polished final definition of *fairy tale*.

ONE CLASS'S IDEAS ABOUT FAIRY TALES

Often, but not always, something magic

A short story

A lot of them have tests

Predictable beginnings and endings

Unlikely to *really* happen

Make-believe

Often have magical helpers

Sometimes scary

Usually starts off not too good and ends up good for main character

Often going somewhere

Nice inside/bad-looking outside

Teaches bad guys a lesson and reader/listener

Has a moral

Significance of parents

Teaches kids what is wrong or right

CINDERELLA PROJECT

ow students are ready to create their own versions of *Cinderella*. Having encouraged video, illustrative, and performance projects during other units, I emphasize writing for this one. In fact, the assignment is for each student to create an original *Cinderella* to contribute to a class *Cindy Book*.

I emphasize the process of writing throughout this project. That is, students begin thinking through the sort of story they want to write. This involves some planning. I provide a variety of graphic organizers for this. Students then begin drafting their stories. I confer with them, and they with one another, and we discuss different aspects of story writing including leads, settings, character development, story grammars, and more. For all that students want to write fantasy, it isn't easy at all. I prepared the chart shown on page 59 to help one class begin this challenging project, and I've found that the Cindy worksheet described below is also helpful to students.

WRITING CINDY STORIES: THE CINDY WORKSHEET

Planning

I designed a worksheet to help students plan their Cindy stories (see page 60). I followed these steps to help them analyze existing stories and then plan their own.

1. I first enlarged the worksheet and used it with the whole class to analyze a published Cinderella story. We used all we knew about Cinderella stories in this activity.

OUTLINING CINDY STORIES

Audience:

classmates, parents, relatives, teachers

Title:

Beginning:

Where is it taking place?
When?
Who? (main character's name and physical description)
What?
Why?
Starting event (e.g., father's remarriage, mother's death)

Middle:

Conflicts (e.g., mean siblings)
Problems (e.g., getting to ball, dress, etc.)

End:

Test
"Ball"
"Marriage"
Problems solved
Moral

What Cinderella Tale Type is yours?:

A. Cinderella is mistreated and there is a shoe test.

B. Princess Furball, where she has to run away from her father.

C. How Much Do You Love Me? When she is the youngest sister of three who loves her father "as meat loves salt."

2. Students then worked in pairs to analyze a picture book Cinderella of their choice using the worksheet. In some cases, students had to adjust the worksheet to fit the story. For example, in some stories, Cinderella starts out poor and mistreated; there is nothing to indicate how she got that way. And some stories, such as Huck's *Princess Furball*, are quite different from the more familiar Perrault version. However, we found that the worksheet did not need too many alterations, even for the less familiar variants.

3. As a class, we shared what we had discovered from the worksheet activity. We decided that the following elements were generally necessary for a story to be a Cinderella story: a change in status for the protagonist, some sort of special help (usually, but not always by way of a magical helper), a special event (such as a ball), and an identity test (often, but not always involving a shoe).

4. Finally students used the same worksheet to plan their own stories.

Students used this plan successfully to help them write their first drafts.

Revising

Once students draft their original stories, they begin the hard work of revision. In the past I encouraged revision by holding brief conferences during the workshop time, by reading and writing comments on drafts and returning them the next day, and by having students meet with peers for feedback. However, recently I tried a different method based on my own experience in a writing class. At the end of each writing period, students who are

Name _____   Date _____

Cindy Story Analysis

Author _____
Title _____

Cinderella Character

Physical Traits

_____
_____

Personality Traits

_____
_____

Other Significant Characters (father, mother, stepmother, stepsisters/brothers, magical helper, prince/princess, etc.)

_____
_____
_____
_____

Setting (When, where, special details, etc.)

_____
_____
_____

Initial Situation (including any events that cause main character's change in status)

_____
_____

Special Event
Introduction of Special Event (often in the form of an invitation)

_____
_____
_____

Main character can't go—why?

_____

_____

_____

Main character gets to go to event—how?

_____

_____

_____

Event and what happens there

_____

_____

_____

_____

Main character leaves event suddenly—why?

_____

_____

_____

_____

Loses something—what?
Rest of family returns from events—what is that like?

_____

_____

_____

_____

Identity Test (shoe or something else)

_____

_____

_____

_____

Resolution (e.g., wedding, becoming a star, living happily ever after, forgiving or not, what happens to the mean family members, etc.)

_____

_____

_____

_____

ready for feedback leave their folders on my desk. I read them and write comments on separate stick-on notes. At the beginning of the next class, I read aloud a portion of one of these works-in-progress to the class. (Those who do not want their works read indicate this when they hand them to me. However, most of my students do want their works read.) The authors are not identified, allowing us to focus closely on the story itself. After my reading, students give their comments; then I follow with mine. The authors, I have discovered, listen carefully and generally do make revisions based on these comments. In fact, I've found that they are more willing to revise with this method than they were when they got feedback in peer conferences. I believe this is because when their work is read anonymously to the class they are able to focus on the story, whereas in peer conferences social dynamics take precedence.

I also conduct mini-lessons focusing on craft. For example, one year I noticed that many students were struggling with transitions. To help them I read aloud the charming picture book *Meanwhile* by Jules Feiffer (HarperColllins, 1997). It helped them to think directly about transitions and how to manage them with greater success. Another mini-lesson resulted in a list of revision techniques different students had discovered with my help.

Revision Strategies for Cindy Stories

The Olivia Technique for Animal Personification Stories
Use animal-related words. For example: Dogs bark, yip, or whine.

The Maggie Technique
- Establish WHY there is a particular sort of test.
- Think about your theme. For example: if your theme is yo-yos, there has to be a good reason for a yo-yo test.

The Brent-Lauren Technique
Don't forget about the father.

The Sarah W Technique
Be careful not to switch tenses.

The Sam Technique
Try to think about how you can expand certain parts.

Everyone's Techniques on Transitions
Try these transition words:
    The next day….
    Later….
    Soon…
    Meanwhile…
    A few weeks later….
    Once the night…
    At the time….

It has been fascinating to observe the different directions students have taken with their stories. Many stay with the familiar trope, complete with fairy-godmother figure and shoe test. Sometimes, however, students choose to take less-known paths and create stories involving tests of character. One year I had a class full of television addicts. I gave them an open invitation to use characters from their favorite shows in their stories. The result were *Saved by the Bell* and *Beverly Hills 90210* variants. The latter inspired one child to write of Brenda wanting to go to a beach party but not having a bikini to wear. Fortunately, it is provided by a fairy godmother. The final test object is Brenda's hair ornament. Another story involved sibling rivalry between Bart and Lisa Simpson. Still another involved a rich stepmother who shopped all day. The

One class's published collection of
Cindy stories

read a favorite variant by someone else.
Once a student wrote a lengthy play called
The Three Princesses. She and her friends
had a wonderful time performing part of it
before the assembled guests. A grand time
was had by all!

FINAL THOUGHTS

Cinderella continues to be a
compelling tale, one that seems so
universal. Every year more and
more variants are produced, both for
children and adults. This universality is
what makes it so appealing as the center of a
thematic study. Students can go far and
wide with such a unit. They can dig deep
into it from so many different places. Other
fairy tales, while perhaps less universal, can
be great for thematic studies as well. One
that a colleague used successfully with his
class is *Beauty and the Beast*. Just think:
Frankenstein, *King Kong*—the possibilities
are most intriguing! Whatever tale you use,
it is bound to stimulate you and your
students to dig deep into genre and theme.

Cinderella character used the stepmother's
American Express card to get her clothes
for the disco.

THE *CINDY* CELEBRATION

Students need an opportunity to
present their work to an audience.
A great way to do this is with a
reading. Once everyone has finished writing
their Cindy story, we compile them in a
Cindy book and invite parents and friends to
a *Cindy* celebration. One year, refreshments
included an enormous Rice Krispie treat in
the shape of a slipper and slipper cookies.
We display charts, books, art, and the like
throughout the room, and each student
makes a brief presentation. Most read
excerpts from their stories. Some choose to

Baseballella

by Matthew Spiro

Once upon a time there was a baseball team called the Hoppin Jalapenos. They were an expansion team, they were considered the worst team in the league, expected to go 0-15, pretty bad huh! All the other teams teased them, especially the defending champs, the High Hawks. . . .

It was the day of the championship. The whole team was in the locker room. All of a sudden they heard a click. They were locked in! There were ten minutes left till game time, they were still locked in! All of a sudden there was a flash! Five seconds later standing right in front of them was Mickey Mantle! Not one could believe their eyes. Then Mickey said, "Do you want to go and play?"

"Yes," the team said. Just like that Mickey swung his golden bat and ... the whole team had new uniforms, new cleats, and golden gloves.

Then Mickey said, "Be back in the locker room right after the game because everything will disappear." With one minute left till game time, Mickey swung his bat and knocked the door down. The Jalapenos took the field just in time. . . .

They won the championship!! They were definitely the best expansion team ever in the league. With no time to celebrate, they dropped their mitts, and ran into the locker room.

One week later it was time for the trophy ceremony. Everyone was excited. Since the champs had fled from the scene, a lot of people were claiming to be on the Jalapenos so they could get the trophy. The league officials couldn't find the list of the teams, and who was on them. Since the champs had left their gloves on the diamond, the league officials had every person in the league (they did have the league register) try on the gloves.

Once they had the Jalapenos all together, they gave them the trophy. Even though the Hawks teased them they still gave them a second place banner.

They have never lost a game since then!

Cinderella Goes to CAMP!

by Erica Bromley

There once was a little girl who lived with her father in a town in New Jersey. The girl's name was Ella and she was 7. She loved her father very much but her father was very sick. Her father died when he was 47, when Ella had just turned 8. Ella went to live with her aunt and cousins in New York. Ella's cousins' names were Elizabeth and Rose. They were twins, they were nice to her when her father was around but they were mean to her now.

When Ella was 9 her aunt sent Ella and her cousins to sleepaway camp for the summer. Ella was in Elizabeth and Rose's bunk and she was really disappointed. . . .

Finally it was Saturday the day it was night swim. Ella's cousins got into their bathing suits and got ready to go down to the lake. When everyone was ready to go Ella's cousins locked her in the SMELLY bathroom, but when they were walking to swim Ella's counselors asked Elizabeth and Rose where Ella was. They said, "I don't know." but really they did. . . .

So 12 years later Ella and Charlie got married and became directors of the camp. And they all lived happily ever after, except for the cousins. Who knows what happened to them!!

Shoerella

by Anna Monaco

Once upon a time there was a shoe named Ella. She was a very kind-hearted shoe and she was very energetic. When Ella was very young her mother died from athlete's foot and after that she was very very sad. So her father went to war for a year, then came back and married a female shoe named Tabitha. Tabitha had two ugly, annoying, selfish, conceited, well I could go on and on about them, but why don't we just get on with the story. . . .

After they left (for the ball) Ella went to the kitchen to get something to eat when all of a sudden there was a big crash and the sound of glass breaking. When Ella opened her eyes she saw a glass shoe. "Darn, I broke my heel."

"Who are you?"

"I am your father's mother's cousin's brother's fairy glass slipper."

Cinderella Poem

by Anne Kurtz

Come and enjoy your stay with us on our adventure to the palace and let's find out about how Cinderella is doing. Cinderella has been enjoying herself a lot more than she has in the past.

In the palace is a very active place. But even though they are very busy they still hold balls and Cinderella invites her step sisters and stepmother.

Never in Cinderella's life did she think that she would marry the prince. Even though she did want to marry the prince a little bit.

Decisions are very important in the palace for instance a dress, what to drink, what to eat, what to do.

Every person in the town can attend Cinderella's balls.

Really it's not so bad even though sometimes she misses her old family.

Every time Cinderella wants something she gets it but now that that has happened a lot she doesn't like to be treated like that.

Let's look around the house. Cinderella has some of the most expensive things around.

Lots of things are different from the way she used to live. So when she gets homesick she just cries.

Any time you go to Cinderella's house you are welcome because she loves visitors.

A Cinderella Study

"Once upon a time. . . .Happily ever after." These words usually surround the stories we know as fairy tales. For there is no doubt in our minds when we read the words "Once upon a time" that a certain kind of story will follow: a fairy tale. Why is this? What is a fairy tale exactly? Is it different from other kinds of stories? Where do fairy tales come from? Why are they called fairy tales anyway?

To help us define what a fairy tale is we are going to take a close look at one well-known tale, *Cinderella*. It seems like everyone knows that story. "Rags to riches" is a popular theme in movies, books, and television shows. Dreaming of winning the lottery, becoming a movie star, making millions in the stock market are all Cinderella dreams, aren't they? We love to watch a Cinderella team move from the bottom of a league to win the pennant or to watch someone go from childhood poverty to become a multimillionaire music star. I think we all want to be Cinderellas!

While it may seem like *Cinderella* belongs to America, it actually comes from far away. In fact, the oldest Cinderella stories come from Asia and scholars have found hundreds of *Cinderella* tales all over the world. We will be studying some of these variants as well as other offshoots of the tale. There will be picture book Cinderellas, video Cinderellas, movie Cinderellas, rap Cinderellas, poetry Cinderellas, male and female Cinderellas, American Cinderellas, African Cinderellas, German Cinderellas, funny Cinderellas, sad Cinderellas, television Cinderellas, operatic Cinderellas, silly Cinderellas, and many many more!

So let's get started! May the shoe fit!

1. Personal *fairy tale* definitions

Please write your definition of a *fairy tale*. Don't worry about trying to come up with the one "right" definition because there isn't one! Just write down your personal idea of a fairy tale.

_____

_____

_____

_____

_____

_____

2. Memories of *Cinderella*

What is your version of *Cinderella*? We will do a retelling of the tale with all the students in the class contributing elements from their own personal versions. Then we will discuss how each of us got these versions in our heads. Did your grandmother first tell you the tale? Did you read it in a book? Perhaps you got your idea from a movie. Let's find out.

_____

_____

_____

_____

_____

_____

3. Analyses of some *Cinderella* variants

You will be looking at many many different versions. I will also be reading versions to you. To keep track of all the variants please use the chart I will give you. It will serve as a record of all the different *Cinderellas* you study and help you as you begin to create a description of what a *Cinderella* story really is.

4. Now become a storyteller

Before fairy tales were written down, people told them to each other. Chose a non-Cinderella fairy tale. Learn it and practice telling it. We will tell our fairy tales to each other.

5. Now select a favorite *Cinderella* and compare it to the fairy tale you told.

Cinderella _____

Fairy Tale _____

How are they alike?

_____

_____

_____

_____

_____

_____

_____

_____

How are they different?

_____

_____

_____

_____

_____

_____

6. Without looking back at your first definition, write your current definition of fairy tale.

_____

_____

_____

_____

_____

_____

When you finish writing your new definition (not before, please!) take a look at your first definition. We will have a class discussion on whether our ideas of fairy tales have changed from this study and if they have, why.

7. Now that we have studied many, many different *Cinderella* variants it is time for us to come up with the elements or motifs that make up a *Cinderella* story. Clearly all the versions we have been studying have things in common. What are some of those things?

_____

_____

_____

_____

_____

_____

8. Now it is your turn! You will create your own *Cinderella* variant! Select your own genre and style. Your work will be published in a class *Cinderella* book which will be presented at a *Cindy* celebration!

CINDERELLA VARIANTS I HAVE STUDIED

Title	Author Illustrator	Genre (e.g., picture book, video, T.V. show, song, novel, poem)	Setting (e.g., China, 17th–century France, 20th–century New York City)	Personal Response (e.g., did you enjoy it, think it was a good retelling, learned from it)

Using Beloved Classics to Deepen Reading Comprehension • Scholastic Professional Books

Digging Deep into Art: A Study of Alice in Wonderland *and Its Illustrators*

*"...once or twice she had peeped into the book her sister was reading,
but it had no pictures or conversations in it, 'and what is the use of a
book,' thought Alice, 'without pictures or conversations?'"*

—LEWIS CARROLL, *ALICE IN WONDERLAND*

A lice in Wonderland was my favorite book as a child. My father read it
to me, and later I read it again and again on my own. The wildness of
characters like the Cheshire Cat and the Mock Turtle, the witty word play, and the
complete and utterly fantastic nature of Wonderland drew me in time and again.
Tenniel's illustrations had much to do with my adoration; his *Alice* was my *Alice*,
and I couldn't imagine the characters any other way.

My first exposure to other artists' illustrations of *Alice in Wonderland* was at the British Library in London, where I saw Lewis Carroll's original manuscript for the story, *Alice's Adventures Underground*. He did his own illustrations, and they were nothing like Tenniel's. Carroll's Alice was a dark-haired pre-Raphaelite, a direct contrast to Tenniel's little blond in a pinafore. During my NEH seminar at Princeton in 1990, I did research on the illustrators of *Alice in Wonderland*. To my delight, I found a myriad of wonderful illustrators of the book. It turned out that illustrating *Alice in Wonderland* was the pinnacle of many an artist's career. A variety of well-known illustrators have attempted Carroll's book; it seems to be like *Hamlet* is for actors—all the greats attempt it. Studying the many different ways illustrators have approached *Alice in Wonderland* makes for a fascinating literature unit.

DIGGING DEEP INTO ART

It used to be that children and teachers alike tended to dismiss illustrated books beyond a certain grade level. The focus became the words all by themselves. Certainly, textbooks had illustrations in them, but little attention was paid to them in their own right (they were usually just used to help with comprehension). However, in recent years illustration has become more and more respected and studied at all grade levels. There are many picture books created today that are geared more to upper elementary grades. Many beautiful editions of beloved classics are being reissued or new ones created. As a result, more and more teachers are highlighting illustrators and illustrations in their classroom literature studies. Indeed, a close look at one illustrator's work over time or a close look at how different illustrators have interpreted the same story is another exciting way to dig deep into literature.

VISUALIZING ALICE

It is January and my students trickle back into the classroom, quite happy to be back in school after a long vacation. After checking in with each other, "Those new shoes—not bad!," "Hey, a Star Wars folder—neat!," "You got a haircut!," they begin to look around the room. "Oh, cool, you've redecorated!" Indeed, editions of *Alice's Adventures in Wonderland* have taken over the display rack. A stuffed Cheshire Cat smirks nearby. The literature bulletin board is now full of Carrollian stuff—photos by and of Lewis Carroll, cartoons playing off the familiar characters of Wonderland, postcards of Oxford, a previous student's map of Wonderland, Disney memorabilia, and more.

"Okay, let's get started!" The children settle into their regular morning routine— a meeting on the rug. After taking attendance, chatting with the class about the break, and reviewing the day's schedule, I begin, "So, by now I suppose you all know my favorite book?"

"*Alice in Wonderland!*" is the chorused answer. Students have known all year that they would be studying the book. They had seen the Wonderland figurines on my desk and had students from years past regale them with memories of the unit and how much I loved the book before ever entering my classroom. Now the time was at hand. They were curious—what would Wonderland be like?

"But of course! I'd be disappointed if you didn't know that about me by now. Anyway, we are indeed finally starting The Many Faces of Alice unit. Tell me, what do you know about this story?"

"I love the Disney movie!"

"A girl falls down a rabbit hole."

" My favorite character is the Cheshire Cat."

"Nothing. It is brand new to me."

"Excellent all! As you know, I'm a big advocate of rereading books, so those of you who, like me, are already familiar with the story should enjoy this revisit. And for those who don't know it at all—you are in for a treat. We'll start by my reading the book aloud to you while you follow along in these different illustrated editions. I'll use an annotated version so that I can point out some cool things as we go along. For example, there are many funny songs and poems in the book which are parodies of popular songs and poems of Carroll's day. Also, the story was first told to a real little girl named Alice Liddell and it is fun to learn about her, too. At the end of each chapter each of you will select your favorite illustrations to share with the class. Soon you will all be experts on both the story and its many illustrators.

"Once we have finished the book you'll get to do your own illustrations! So, let's get started. Go wash your hands, pick a book, and settle down to hear all about Alice's amazing adventures!"

Despite constant references to *Alice in Wonderland* few people today seem to have any direct experience with the book. Like my students, they often only know it from the Disney movie, or vaguely as a book that may well be too sophisticated for middle-grade readers today. It is easy to forget when political pundits make mention of Tweedledum-Tweedledee Democrats (to give one recent example during the 2000 presidential campaign) that this is a story originally told to a real little girl and emphatically written by its creator for children. Lewis Carroll was tired of the rather stern children's books available in Victorian England and wanted to write something different; a book with a cranky, imperfect heroine, without a moral, but with wit and humor. Certainly, today Wonderland can seem like a very strange place, appropriate because Carroll meant it to be a dream with all the weirdness that entails. Yet peculiar as the inhabitants of Wonderland may be, none are truly frightening. Indeed, none of them can compare to the truly terrifying

Voldemort of the Harry Potter books to which *Alice in Wonderland* is often compared. The most threatening character in Wonderland is the execution-happy Queen of Hearts, and Alice, most sensibly, has figured that she is mostly bluster and not someone to worry about. In fact, one of the amusing aspects of the book is the way Alice, a little girl, often appears larger and more fearful to the characters than they are to her. With the enthusiasm for fantasy literature at a high due to the enormous popularity of the Harry Potter books, earlier fantasy books like *Alice in Wonderland* are being reintroduced to children today.

LEWIS CARROLL

ewis Carroll was a rather eccentric Englishman, a mathematics instructor and clergyman at Christ Church College in Oxford. He was born in 1832 as Charles Lutwidge Dodgson, the eldest of eleven children. Even as a child his talent was evident as he clearly enjoyed entertaining his younger siblings with stories and games. As an adult he became an amateur photographer as well as a writer of mathematical books. A shy man due to a stammer, he never married, although he developed close attachments to a number of young girls over the years. While this may give us pause today, his affections were not atypical for Victorians. There is not a shred of evidence that his interactions with children were anything but appropriate.

While Carroll had many child friends in the course of his life, one of his favorites was certainly Alice Liddell, the little girl to whom he initially told the *Alice* stories. He first told the story on a lazy rowboat outing on a warm summer afternoon. Eventually he wrote the story down and showed it to some friends who encouraged him to publish it. He did so, and the book was a raging success. It prompted him to do a nursery version, to oversee theatrical versions, to produce toys related to the book (Disney did not invent the tie-in), and finally to write a sequel, *Alice Through the Looking-glass*.

Carroll wrote several other children's books; however, none was as successful as the two *Alice* books. He died in 1898.

THE *ALICE* CENTER

efore beginning this unit I set up an *Alice* center in my classroom. It consists of many different illustrated editions of *Alice in Wonderland* as well as other material related to the story, the author, and the period. I constantly come across cartoons, headlines, and ads that refer to *Alice*. I keep these and display them in the center. As we get more and more involved in the unit, my students add their own books.

MEMORIES OF *ALICE* IN *WONDERLAND*

 begin, as always, with memories. I tell my students my experiences with the story and they tell me theirs. Rarely do I find that they have had direct exposure to the book. More commonly, they have seen the Disney film or an adapted stage version. Sometimes they have performed in it themselves.

READING ALOUD *ALICE* IN *WONDERLAND*

lice in Wonderland is best read aloud by an adult. Most of the book is dialogue that will be much more enjoyable for your students if you read it. The vocabulary is difficult and there are many Briticisms in the book. Reading it to your class means that they can focus on the content of the book rather than the mechanics of decoding. I encourage my students to follow along as I read, but whether or not you wish to do so depends on your particular class. What is most important is that students get a sense of the humor and language of the book.

I read from *The Annotated Alice* with notes by Martin Gardner. Much of the book is better appreciated with some background, and Gardner's notes are comprehensive. For example, most of the poems are parodies of serious poems or songs of Carroll's day. Children in those days were expected to stand before adults and recite poems. Most of these poems taught lessons of good virtue. Thus, "How doth the little crocodile" plays wickedly with the most earnest poem "How doth the little busy bee." Reading a few stanzas of the original poem helps my students appreciate Carroll's humor. I point out some of the mathematical puzzles if the children seem agreeable. I am careful with these interruptions. Too many, and my students will lose interest in the story.

STUDYING THE ILLUSTRATIONS

 provide my students with many different illustrated editions of *Alice*. In addition to interruptions for context information, we also stop to study the different illustrators. Students become adept at noting the different approaches to illustrations very quickly. For example, Alice is represented in many different ways. Some illustrators keep to an Alice similar to Tenniel's. Others make Alice look more like photographs of the real Alice Liddell. Some doting fathers, like Barry Moser and Michael Hague, use their own daughters as Alice models. It is interesting to see what is actually illustrated. Since everything is so wild in Wonderland, some illustrators avoid certain scenes. Disney cut the Pig Baby out of his movie completely, and his and others' avoid the Duchess's kitchen, perhaps because beating a baby no longer seems particularly humorous. A number of illustrators have commented on contemporary issues within their drawings. Tenniel was a political cartoonist, and there is much speculation that certain characters are prominent politicians of his day. Ralph Steadman makes the playing cards into union cards, and Barry Moser has a March Hare that looks remarkably like Ringo Starr.

RESPONDING TO THE BOOK

 set aside a special *Alice* time every day for the class. Preparation includes washing hands as my students learn to handle the books as one does works of art. The books are from my own collection, and students are thrilled that I am allowing them to handle them. They have always taken very good care of my books. As we read we also discuss the book. Usually we review the previous day's reading before going on.

In any class, some students are more verbal than others. I ask my students to respond to the book in their journals as well as during class discussions. The journal responses often reveal that readers who did not appear to be interested were actually quite engaged by the book.

QUESTIONS TO PONDER

nce I have finished the book I ask my students to answer the following questions in their journals.

How did you like the book?

Is it a fairy tale? Why or why not?

Is it like Cinderella? *Why or why not?*

Who was your favorite character and why?

Who was your favorite illustrator and why?

STUDENT JOURNAL RESPONSES TO THE BOOK

My feelings for the book have changed a lot. In the beginning I hated the story and plot, but now looking at it from a different point of view it is a very funny book. (especially the way Lewis Carroll writes it.)

Anna Monaco

Alice was a *great* story! I never knew it could be this good if you read it aloud. I have never read an unabridged version, but now I have because you showed it to me. Now I am almost finished with *Through the Looking-glass.* I think that both of these books are great. Although *Alice in Wonderland* I find a little better because Alice is doing more and finding more and more interesting things.

Jody Shechtman

CLASS DISCUSSIONS

Several class discussions follow, based on journal responses. I usually create a class chart such as the following during these discussions. This gives us a permanent record of the group's ideas about the book.

CLASS CHART ON *ALICE IN WONDERLAND*

Is it a fairy tale?

Yes,
- because it is magical;
- you don't know it is a dream until the end;
- it is unreal;
- it is imaginative;
- it is make-believe;
- it has magical animals and magical people.

It is like *Cinderella* because:

- The test was for Alice to get to the garden.
- Alice has sisters and so does Cinderella.
- The King and Queen act like Cinderella's stepmother.
- The court case or croquet game is like Cinderella's "ball."
- Alice and Cinderella are both girls.
- There are animals in both stories.
- Cinderella and Alice sometimes have similar personalities.

Favorite characters:

- White Rabbit
- Mock Turtle
- Queen
- Mad Hatter
- March Hare
- Cheshire Cat
- Dormouse
- Alice
- Griffin
- Hedgehog and Flamingo

Favorite illustrators:

- Anthony Browne
- William Bradley
- John Tenniel
- Mervyn Peake
- Barry Moser
- Lewis Carroll

DENNIS POTTER'S *DREAMCHILD*

reamchild is a British film by Dennis Potter. It is a fictionalized account of a trip that Mrs. Alice Hargraves (née Liddell) took to New York City on the centenary of Lewis Carroll's birth. Although Mrs. Hargraves did indeed travel to New York, most of the film is pure fantasy. It has the elderly Mrs. Hargraves trying to think back to her childhood and experiences with Lewis Carroll. At the same time she is haunted by characters from Wonderland. A subplot involves a romance between her young companion and a brash New York journalist.

STUDENT JOURNAL RESPONSES TO *DREAMCHILD*

I liked *Dreamchild* very much. I liked it because it wasn't so "kiddish." Some other "classic" movies I saw made me feel *sick*. Not because they were disgusting, it was because they were so *hammy*.

Eric Kiung

Dreamchild was great!

Recommended by me.

Enjoy the flashbacks.

Alice is confused because she doesn't understand.

Mrs. Hargraves is nice when you get to know her.

Charles Dodgson wants to marry Alice, but she doesn't realize it.

Happily, lively Alice doesn't take Mr. Dodgson seriously.

Interesting and makes you understand *Alice in Wonderland* better.

Lewis Carroll's real name is Charles Dodgson.

Does Alice start to understand at the end?

Rachel Rosenthal

DISNEY'S *ALICE IN WONDERLAND*

ne year, for the first time, I decided to show the Disney film. It came up more often then usual in our discussions and I got a copy on sale.

The children were struck by how much of *Through the Looking-glass* was in the film. They also noted the great difference in the ending. In the book, Wonderland is clearly a dream while Disney's version has Alice running away from the court scene at the end. Disney's Wonderland is no dream.

STUDENT JOURNAL RESPONSES TO DISNEY'S *ALICE IN WONDERLAND*

I liked the movie a lot but they skipped my favorite parts, like the Mock Turtle. I would have liked to see what it would have looked like. They had her going through the looking-glass in the Disney version of *Alice in Wonderland*.

Disney had a good idea of mixing the two together to make one and it turned out pretty good. I especially liked the Walrus and the Carpenter in the Disney movie. In the movie I think Alice should have had brown or black hair because that's the way Lewis Carroll saw her and that's how she really looked (the real Alice Liddell).

The idea of scrambling up sentences and making them go with different people (or should I say "things") was a good idea to make it shorter.

In all I liked them both a lot, the Disney movie and the Lewis Carroll version.

Mack Cauley

I really liked Disney's *Alice in Wonderland* because I think its really well fixed up for small children. Disney made half of the movie up because the wood doesn't have any of the ducks, vultures, momraths, or any of the other weird animals. Disney teaches a lesson and makes her seem grown up, but in Carroll he *doesn't* want Alice to grow up, because he wanted to marry her when she grew a little older.

Sarah Wertheimer

A CLASS COMPARISON OF CARROLL AND DISNEY

A class discussion focused on the similarities and differences between the book and the Disney film produced the following chart.

CLASS CHART COMPARING CARROLL'S *ALICE* AND DISNEY'S *ALICE*

❈ Disney took poems and adages from one character and gave them to others. (e.g., unbirthday from Humpty Dumpty to March Hare and Mad Hatter).

❈ Disney scene in woods seemed new although it referred to "Jabberwocky."

❈ Disney gives much more of a quest for Alice to go home while Carroll just has her trying to get to the garden.

❈ Disney's garden is very scary while Carroll's is interesting.

❈ Disney: Alice tries to wake up.

❈ Carroll: Sister wakes Alice up.

❈ Disney's is confusing because it mixes up two stories.

❈ Disney changes order of events and adds stuff.

❈ Disney left out the Duchess, the key into the garden, the Pig Baby, the Mock Turtle and Griffin.

❈ Disney added from *Looking-glass* Tweedledum and Tweedledee, unbirthday, talking flowers, Jabberwocky, woods

❈ Disney: Alice learns a lesson: no more nonsense. She seems older. Grows up during the movie. Wiser by the end. Is on a quest/journey.

❈ Carroll: There is no lesson. Not as serious. Alice is seven and a half. Carroll doesn't want her to grow up.

Using Beloved Classics to Deepen Reading Comprehension • Scholastic Professional Books

ALICE PROJECT

very year the culminating project for this unit has been for students to create their own Alice illustrations. I spend a lot of time talking about the different media and ways to approach the project. While most children choose to do a series of illustrations there have been others who preferred to create one large poster full of scenes from the book. Those who feel they can't draw have used collage and computer art programs with great success. One year two of my students created Wonderland stuffed animals. One was a most "cool" caterpillar and the other a delightful Cheshire Cat, with a caption from the story on his stomach. Some of the most delightful written pieces have placed the Wonderland characters in different contexts. Thus, one child had Alice falling into a manhole in New York City while another had her falling down an elevator shaft. Two diehard fans had great fun sending Alice to Baseball Land (aka Yankee Stadium) via the subway—what else?

THE MANY FACES OF ALICE WEB SITE

s the Web started to become more and more popular, I began wondering if I could put the children's illustrations on the Internet. In 1998 and 1999 this dream became a reality with the Many Faces of Alice project.

For many years I had been participating in a children's literature discussion group on the Internet and had come across Roxanne Feldman, a New York City librarian who loved *Alice* as much as I did. We finally met at a conference and before long she came to my school as a librarian. Roxanne had already created a well-known children's literature web site and was excited at the idea of creating a

Web-based *Alice* project with my class. Joined by Eileen Gumport, a computer specialist at my school, we created The Many Faces of Alice web site.

While I initially thought we would just put a few illustrations on the Web, with Roxanne and Eileen's tutelage I discovered that much more was possible. It turned out we could create a complete *Alice in Wonderland* of our own. Roxanne found a copy of the text (which is out of copyright and thus available to anyone) and divided it into Web pages: six per chapter. We then paired the children up, two to a chapter. For each

One student's Alice project illustration

"Well! I've often seen a cat without a grin," thought Alice; "But a grin without a cat! It's the most curious thing I ever saw in my life!"

chapter they created illustrations, annotations, and essays about the whole experience. Roxanne designed the site, while Eileen worked with the children so they learned how to create Web pages themselves. It was such an exhilarating experience that we repeated it with the 1999 class. The Many Faces of Alice can be viewed at www.dalton.org/alice.

An illustration from the Alice project

THE *ALICE IN WONDERLAND* TEA PARTY

ne year a group of children asked if we could do a Mad Hatter tea party. I thought it was a great idea, a wonderful way to celebrate our time with Alice. On the day of the tea party I transformed the classroom into the Mad Hatter's garden. I moved all the desks together and covered them with table clothes. The children had provided many tasty tea treats such as scones, biscuits, teacakes, and more. I provided the tea. It was a wonderful event. Many of the children dressed up as Wonderland characters. Over tea they shared their illustrations and then we watched the Disney film. It was an interesting experience now that the children were experts on the book itself. Now, the Alice Tea Party has become a yearly event, always a bit different, but always great fun!

Students in costume for the Alice party.

FINAL THOUGHTS

ear after year I have been amazed by my students' responses to the *Alice* unit. While I anticipate the enjoyment of my high-level readers, it's my weaker readers who most surprise me. These literal thinkers who might be expected to find the story difficult to follow are often the most enthusiastic of all. I think reading the book aloud, providing some background and context for it, and showing the multiple illustrated versions make *Alice* pleasurable for everyone. Class discussions, written responses, and the students' final illustrations prove that the children not only enjoy the book, but also are able to interpret it in quite sophisticated ways. At the end of every year I ask my students what their favorite literature unit was. The majority always answer, The Many Faces of Alice.

STUDENT PACKET
THE MANY FACES OF *ALICE*

INTRODUCTION

One of the most well-known books for children is *Alice in Wonderland*. It was written well over 100 years ago in England yet remains remarkably popular all over the world. Just as fairy tales like *Cinderella* began as tales told by storytellers, so did *Alice in Wonderland* begin as a series of stories told by Lewis Carroll to Alice Liddell and her two sisters. Eventually, just as the most well known fairy tales were written down and published in books, so did Lewis Carroll write down his stories into what we now know as *Alice in Wonderland*. If you have not yet read (or heard) the real *Alice in Wonderland*, then you are in for a treat. It is imaginative, crazy, funny, clever, and wild all at the same time. Enjoy!

Our study of *Alice in Wonderland* will focus on the following:

❀ Pure enjoyment of the book!

  I will read this book to you, so you may read along if you wish or simply sit back and listen.

❀ A closer look at the puns, puzzles, and jokes in the book

Lewis Carroll was a mathematician and threw in all kinds of puzzles in the book. He also loved puns (word plays) and making fun of popular activities of his day.

❀ The life and times of Lewis Carroll

Lewis Carroll was a fascinating, brilliant man. In addition to being a scholar at Oxford University, he was a photographer and a minister.

❀ A close study of the many illustrators of *Alice in Wonderland*

While you may know the Tenniel illustrations best, you will be intrigued by the many other illustrators of the book. The story is so well known that everyone seems to want to illustrate it. You will see how the book has been illustrated in different times, countries, and media.

LEWIS CARROLL

Lewis Carroll's real name was Charles Lutwidge Dodgson. He spent most of his life at Oxford University, England, teaching mathematics. Apparently he wasn't a great teacher; his classes were known to be dull and boring. Although we know him best as the author of the *Alice* books, he also wrote books about mathematics. Quite shy as an adult, he was most comfortable with children, especially little girls. Alice Liddell was his most famous child friend, but he had many throughout his life. He stuttered when nervous; perhaps that is why he seems to have been more comfortable with children than with adults. In addition to writing mathematics books and creating fantasy stories, Lewis Carroll enjoyed photography. Many of his photos of child friends remain. Certainly, there are many of Alice Liddell.

After the publication of *Alice in Wonderland* and *Alice Through the Looking-glass*, Carroll wrote other books for children. Unfortunately, they were not as good as the *Alice* books and are only of interest to Carroll scholars today.

Lewis Carroll died on January 14, 1898.

THE CREATION OF
ALICE IN WONDERLAND

Alice in Wonderland began as a story told on a boat trip. Lewis Carroll and his friend, the Reverend Robinson Duckworth, took the three Liddell girls out on the Thames River on July 4, 1862. The three girls were Lorina, age 13, Alice, age 10, and Edith, age 8. Carroll wrote about the expedition in his diary and later added a note that it was then that he had told the story of Alice's adventures underground.

Alice so enjoyed the story that Carroll decided to write it down for her. (Remember, this was before typewriters or computers.) He finally presented her with *Alice's Adventures Underground* on November 26, 1864. The book was beautifully handwritten with illustrations by Lewis Carroll himself.

Before Carroll gave the book to Alice, he showed it to some friends who felt he should publish it. So he revised the book, changed parts, added parts, and found John Tenniel to do the illustrations. The book we know today, *Alice in Wonderland*, came out in 1865. It was a huge success. Before long it was known throughout the world. There are people today who collect *Alices* from all over the world. One collector had *Alices* in 125 different languages!

ILLUSTRATORS OF
ALICE IN WONDERLAND

The very first illustrator of *Alice* was Lewis Carroll himself. Since he was not a professional illustrator, when he decided to publish the book he looked for a well-known illustrator. John Tenniel was a popular cartoonist; *Alice* was his first children's book. Carroll worked closely with Tenniel to see that the illustrations were just as he wanted them. Tenniel also illustrated *Alice Through the Looking-glass.* Throughout Lewis Carroll's life, he and Tenniel were the only published illustrators of the book.

After Lewis Carroll died, other well-known illustrators attempted to illustrate the book. One of the first, Arthur Rackham, was already well known. Over the years, many others have attempted to illustrate the book. Alice has been presented as a 1920s flapper, as an African-American, and as an Australian aboriginal. Every artist who takes on Wonderland makes it their own. Hopefully, you will too.

MEMORIES OF *ALICE IN WONDERLAND*

What do you know of this book? Perhaps you saw the Disney cartoon or acted in a play version? Did you ever read it or have it read to you? Perhaps you just vaguely know about it; that's just fine too. Write down what you know of *Alice in Wonderland* here.

_____

_____

_____

_____

_____

_____

_____

_____

_____

READING
ALICE IN WONDERLAND

I will read this book to you. You will listen or follow along in one of the different illustrated editions. We will need to rotate the different versions through the class so everyone has a chance to look at them. It is important to handle these books carefully. Begin with clean hands and be careful as you turn pages. They are works of art and deserve your gentle care.

As I read the book to you, we will stop when necessary to look at illustrations, to consider why different artists made the choices they made regarding what they illustrated and didn't, and how they illustrated parts of the book. We will also interrupt the reading to discuss the puzzles and jokes in the book. How often we stop will depend on what the class wishes. For example, if the class would rather wait till the end of a chapter before looking at all the illustrations, that is what we will do. Each class I've worked with has had its own way of doing it. I will respect the way this particular class wishes to approach the reading, the illustrations, and the discussion.

RESPONDING TO
ALICE IN WONDERLAND

You will be asked both during and at the end of the readings to respond in your journal to the book and whatever comes up in discussions as we study the text and the illustrations.

QUESTIONS TO PONDER
AFTER READING
ALICE IN WONDERLAND

How did you like the book?

_____

_____

_____

_____

_____

Is it a fairy tale? Why or why not?

_____

_____

_____

_____

_____

Which character did you like best and why?

_____

_____

_____

_____

Which illustrator did you like best and why?

_____

_____

_____

_____

_____

_____

FINAL *ALICE IN WONDERLAND* PROJECT

Now that you have seen what all those other artists did, you are going to do your own illustrations of *Alice in Wonderland*! Think carefully about what scenes you want to illustrate, what materials you wish to use, etc. Be creative and have fun! Remember not only all the different ways this book has been illustrated, but all the ways traditional fairy tales are approached by writers, filmmakers, and artists. Your path is wide open!

Digging Deep into Film: A Comparative Study of The Wizard of Oz—Baum's Book and the MGM Movie

"...I've done a good deal of thinking, these past three years, about the advantages of a good pair of ruby slippers..."

—Salman Rushdie
BFI Film Classics:
The Wizard of Oz

Television came to my house when I was 8. Even after it was ensconced in our guest room, my sister and I were strictly limited to one hour a day. In order to squeeze in as many programs as possible we left the room for commercials. The way we figured it, that gave us three programs.

The one-hour rule was lifted for special events such as the yearly showing of *The Wizard of Oz*. That was an event I looked forward to and savored long after it was over. The TV was black and white so the dramatic switch to color when Dorothy got to Oz was lost to me. It didn't matter, though. I adored it. No other movie had the same effect on me as a child.

Today, my students have a different relationship with television and movies. They zap from program to program, "surfing" the 60-plus cable channels; everything is just the push of a remote control button away. If they like a movie they can rent it or buy it, and view it as often as they wish. Certainly, the dramatic special effects of *The Wizard of Oz* can seem tame in this day of computerized morphing and digitization. Yet, even for these children, *The Wizard of Oz* movie still enthralls. It is part of our popular culture. Who hasn't heard or said, "I don't think we are in Kansas anymore" or "There's no place like home"? Reading, viewing, and studying the film and the original text is fascinating for children, as well as an excellent way to have them consider how a story is transformed in different media.

DIGGING DEEP INTO FILM

 hildren, most agree, are becoming more and more visually oriented every year. Their television viewing, Internet surfing, and computer game playing causes them to be far more visually oriented than previous generations. And I have discovered the uselessness of worrying about how this is causing children to be less and less interested in reading; instead, I've realized it can be a way to get them more interested! Many well-known works of children's literature have been adapted into film. Comparing the original book to the film is yet another stimulating approach to help children dig deep into literature.

Throughout this book I have described my use of video to enhance literature studies. In the Cinderella study I used videos as other versions of the classic tale, alongside picture books and novels. In the Alice study we viewed *Dreamchild,* a lovely consideration of the relationship between the real Alice and Lewis Carroll. However, there are some movies that are known as well as if not better than the original books. Studying the two together can be an intriguing literature unit. And one of the most famous is *The Wizard of Oz.*

AN AMERICAN FAIRY TALE

 Frank Baum wanted *The Wonderful Wizard of Oz* (published in 1900) to be a new kind of fairy tale. He also made it distinctly American. Dorothy is a farm girl from Kansas, and Baum brilliantly contrasts the plain prairies with the extravagant landscapes of Oz. The traditional European fairy tales were full of class issues—princes marrying peasant girls, clever farmers becoming kings, and the like. Wealth was often the reward. Baum, ever the American, turned away from such issues. No one marries in the book, and no one seems very interested in royalty or gaining wealth. The Wicked Witch of the West is the ogre of the story, but Dorothy's only reward for killing her is to go home, to the very same drab, spartan Kansas farm she left at the beginning. She does not go back with material wealth, but with a greater appreciation of her love for her aunt and uncle and their simple life.

Metro-Goldwyn-Mayer's 1939 Film

arly film versions of the book were unsuccessful and forgettable. The MGM film was different. The studio was interested in creating a blockbuster movie, something to compete with Disney's first full-length animated feature, *Snow White and the Seven Dwarfs*. The combination of memorable musical comedy numbers, sterling performances, and special effects made the movie a classic.

A reasonable success when first released, the movie really became known to all when it was televised in the '50s and '60s. Today, most Americans know the story from the movie, not from the book.

Wizard of Oz Memories

his unit begins, as do all my units, with a discussion of students' background knowledge of the book and film. Most students know the film; far fewer know the book. Often they have performed a theatrical version in school or camp. They love to discuss what they know of the movie.

One year I had a student who was reading a number of scary books. He and I were having a wonderful time discussing the books and scary stories in his journal. At one point he mentioned that he and his mother were reading a book together which was so scary that she finished it on her own after he went to bed. I responded that I was always so easily scared as a child that I doubt that I would have been able to read the book. I went on to describe my tremendous fear of Oz's flaming head in the MGM movie. My student was flabbergasted that this scared me. It was mighty tame stuff in his opinion. Today, with the level of violence and terror so

heightened in film and television, 9-year-olds are hard-pressed to find witches and flying monkeys particularly frightening.

The Book

Reading the Book

The Wonderful Wizard of Oz is a book that my fourth graders can read on their own. Baum is a serviceable writer; the content of his book is much more interesting than his actual writing. I have my students read a facsimile version published by Dover so that they can also experience Denslow's original illustrations.

Many of my students find this book one of their favorites of the year. They are fascinated by the landscape of Oz, and the story holds them even if they already know it from the movie. I frequently have children reading through lunch and at every available free moment. It has been especially rewarding to see students who do not normally speak positively about reading talk about "loving" this book. It is a sure-fire hit every time.

Book Talk

My approach to book discussions about *The Wizard of Oz* has changed from year to year. We read it in the spring, so I want to see if students can apply what they have learned in earlier literature studies. That is, can they begin to dig deep into the book, using the techniques we have been using all year, without my explicitly providing them? Each class is different, so I've tried different approaches each year. Sometimes I have asked the class how they would like to discuss the book. As a whole class? In small teacher-led groups? In small student-run groups? Sometimes I want to try a particular method based on my observations of students that year. Each year has been different, but I have always been delighted to see the children successfully begin to use more independently the critical analysis skills they have been introduced to in the course of the year.

TEACHER-LED SMALL-GROUP DISCUSSIONS

One class asked to meet in half-class groups led by me. I divided our reading period into two parts and met with each group for half the time while the other half read. After several meetings, the class asked to have the groups be reformed so that they could hear their peers' thoughts about the book. The ideas they raised were wonderful! One boy noted that the silver slippers (ruby in the movie) were like Cinderella's glass slippers. I found this a fascinating comment since Dorothy seems so unlike Cinderella in other ways. Yet Baum did place the all important magic in those shoes, just as the shoe test in the Cinderella tale is all important to her ultimate happiness. Another student commented that she didn't think the Wicked Witch was really wicked, just greedy. The others in the group animatedly agreed. I was so interested in this idea and tried to see if it was because she didn't kill people. Students were unable to define wickedness for me, only to keep insisting that the witch wasn't. These kinds of comments always stay with me, and I like to bring them up with different groups of students to see if they agree, disagree, or have fresh insights.

STUDENT-LED SMALL-GROUP DISCUSSIONS

Whenever I read and hear about literature circles I am intrigued. Students working in small groups, having serious and deep conversations about books without a teacher to guide them, excites me a lot. However, my experience with literature circles has been mixed. Without me, the skilled reader, there to nudge them into deeper thinking, most groups stay with safe topics, generally basic comprehension questions. They rarely move into the rich sorts of discussions we have as a class. At times one student may attempt to push the group in such a direction, but may be stymied because he or she does not have the social skills to do so without problems arising. However, I continue to experiment with literature circles and have found *The Wizard of Oz* a good book to use for this because it is so accessible to all my students.

I decided to use literature circles with a recent class and began by telling them that they would be reading and discussing *The Wizard of Oz* completely in small groups. They were used to working in small groups in other academic areas but not in literature. This would be a new experience for them and they were very excited. I warned them that it would be a challenge. The faster readers would need to make the slower and less assured readers feel part of the group as well. They would also need to create environments where every participant felt his or her ideas would be valued. It was a tall order that they were most excited about.

To help them get started I asked the whole class to provide a list of tips for small-group study. I typed them up and gave each group a copy; see the sample below.

TIPS FOR SMALL-GROUP LITERATURE STUDY

- Agree/decide on how much to read from one meeting to the next; come in prepared to talk about it.

- Choose a group organizer to lead the discussion so everyone doesn't call out at once. (Can be permanent or change each time, whatever your group decides.)

- Negotiate how much to read so it is fair/comfortable for all.

- Be aware that different people read at different speeds and be sensitive to that.

- Give each group member a number for speaking order.

- Agree on some guiding questions for the group's discussion.

- Decide on a method to record what is said, e.g., tape recording, having one person take notes, having each group member write a summary at the end of the day's discussion, or another idea.

- While reading, write down ideas in a separate notebook or use stickies to annotate.

The first thing I asked each group to do was fill out the following chart:

❧❧❧❧❧❧❧ WIZARD OF OZ ❧❧❧❧❧❧❧

Group Members:
_____
_____
_____

Will you have a group organizer? If so, how will he/she be selected? If not, how will you run your group?

List some guiding questions that your group will use in your reading and discussions.

1. _____
2. _____
3. _____
4. _____

How will you record your discussions?

Tape recording? If so, who will get the recorder and tape?

Note taking? If so, who is taking the notes?

Summaries? If so, who is collecting them?

Any other plans for your group?

Using Beloved Classics to Deepen Reading Comprehension • Scholastic Professional Books

The groups worked unevenly. Some spent most of their time arguing about whose turn it was to speak. Others got along well, but only discussed very basic comprehension questions, finding those safer than the more open-ended kind we had done in whole groups. A couple of groups did touch upon more complex discussions, which pleased me.

Here are some of the notes from their discussions.

"We all agreed that the Wizard did not really give them a brain or a heart or courage. He just made them believe that they had it."

"I like the way that the book just starts. The way that they just get into it."

"I think that Dorothy is a lot nicer than Alice because Alice was very sarcastic. Dorothy was polite and nice all at the same time."

"I don't understand how Dorothy could fall asleep in the middle of a cyclone!"

"I thought the description of the cyclone was very powerful. I think Baum wrote a real page turner."

"If the Scarecrow has no brains how can he talk?"

"Dorothy seems to be happy and optimistic; always sure of things."

"Dorothy went through a wormhole that looked like a tornado and she went to another dimension."

"We agreed that the book is more detailed than the movie. We thought they would be the same."

"Everyone agrees that The Wizard of Oz is a lot scarier than Alice in Wonderland."

"I wouldn't want to go to Oz 'cause it would be dangerous. No, home is better."

"I would want to go to Oz to see a totally different world, but only if I could go home."

"I would ask Oz to go back to New York and be a Knicks player."

"I would ask Oz to be a scientist."

"I would ask Oz to go to Las Vegas and be a singer."

JOURNAL RESPONSES TO THE BOOK

Students always write journal responses during and after reading the book. Here are a few examples.

I like it a lot but I thought it would be a lot different because I've seen the movie so many times and the movie is very different. I think Dorothy and Alice have totally different personalities. Alice is very curious and when she saw the shoes (the silver slippers) she'd probably say something like "Oh what curious things. They are very beautiful. I wish Dinah (her cat) was here. She'd tell me if I should try them on." Dorothy is kind of straightforword. Also, if Alice was called a sorceress she'd be like "How fun it must be to be a sorceress but I'm not one. . . ."

Eli Meltzer

. . . These are a couple of comments I have on both stories: I think that there was a big difference on how rich or poor Dorothy and Alice were. It is obvious that Dorothy's family was not rich. I think Alice was more wealthy because she went to school and everything (lessons). I also think that Dorothy does not have as much character as Alice. But maybe Alice needed more logic to survive in Wonderland.

Eric Kiung

I think *The Wizard of Oz* is very different from *Alice in Wonderland* because Alice just wants to get to the garden because she thinks it's pretty and Dorothy is more reliable because she worries about her aunt and uncle and getting home. I myself like Dorothy better because she isn't selfish like Alice. I like *The Wizard of Oz* better than *Alice in Wonderland* because I like quests and Dorothy is on a quest to find the Wizard of Oz.

Sarah Wertheimer

The Wizard of Oz is really good so far, especially when the bad witches die. The Wicked Witch of the West just died in my book. Now they're going back to the Wizard! I've read the book many times and would say that this time it is the best. I can't wait to see what the end of the book is like again!

Jody Shechtman

I think *The Wizard of Oz* is really great! I like Dorothy better than Alice because she's more common. She seems to care about people more and isn't as bossy as Alice. She is kind of like Wilbur in *Charlotte's Web*. She is humble and doesn't think that much of herself. She thinks everyone is better, nicer, and smarter than her. She seems to deserve a nice land better than Alice does. Since Alice is bossy and can be *VERY* rude, she doesn't deserve all of her adventures other than the one with the queen. It should have taught her a lesson, but all it did was make her even more bossy and self-defensive. Dorothy is very sensitive to other people's feelings and isn't ever rude (at least not so far). I'm really enjoying the book. I can't wait to see what happens. I think its *very* well written. It pulls you in and makes you feel like you're there. I never knew that it was such a good book. This is the best book I've read in a *LONG* time.

Rachel Rosenthal

CHARACTER DESCRIPTIONS

I know that there will be times in my students' educational future where they will be expected to respond to books in more formal ways such as plot summaries, character descriptions, or a setting map. I use *The Wizard of Oz* to expose them to these kinds of writing. We brainstorm the kinds of things that would go into a character description. Sometimes we discuss organizing a character description into two parts: a physical description and a personality description.

Dorothy is a very kind hearted girl. She is so sweet that when she heard she killed the witch she was terrified for she had never in her life killed anyone. Dorothy likes Oz but she wants to get home to her aunt and uncle because she is afraid they will be worried. Dorothy is also very sensitive. She also worried about everything. She keeps her troubles to herself especially when she is with her companions.

Alexandra Saltiel

Dorothy is a very young person not very capable of going outside alone. She is very kind and sweet. Dorothy is very little, is not very smart, and is always thinking of home. She can get very scared at times so she goes on journeys with friends that support her. Her personality is very different. She is very sweet and kind if you hurt yourself then she would try to help you or panic. My example of Dorothy: Dorothy would be able to do lots of things but she really hates *death*. When Dorothy gets mad she really doesn't get that mad because she isn't that kinds of person.

Anne Kurtz

THE FILM

sually my students have seen the movie before. However, they approach the class viewing very differently after having read the book, since it is so different from the movie. Whole sections of the book have been eliminated, Dorothy is much older in the movie, and the whole story is framed as a dream Dorothy has after being knocked out during the tornado. For Baum's Dorothy, Oz is quite real. Certainly, students enjoy analyzing the similarities and differences between the book and the movie as well as their likes and dislikes.

STUDENT RESPONSES AFTER VIEWING THE MGM MOVIE

After students have had sufficient time to read, discuss, and respond to the book, we view the movie. If possible, I recommend either the Fiftieth Anniversary Edition video or the new Collector's Edition. Both have footage of outtakes, home movies, newsreels, and other material related to the movie. My students have especially enjoyed the extended sequence of the Scarecrow's "If I Only Had a Heart." The cut portion includes the Scarecrow flying across the cornfield!

Once we have viewed the movie we discuss it and compare it to the book. We often compare it to more current movies, in terms of scariness and special effects.

I liked both the movie and the book. I think that there were a couple of things about the movie that did not make sense like the Cowardly Lion. The Cowardly Lion never got part of his wish, which was to be the "king of the beasts. . . ." Another part that did not make any sense to me was the part in the movie when Dorothy was riding in the cyclone and saw those people flying by in the window. How could an old lady be knitting when she was in a cyclone?

Eric Kiung

I liked the book better than the movie because the book had more detail. The movie cut out a lot. I can't really blame them, but they cut out a lot of the best parts and they also put in some things that weren't meant to be there. It was like they wrote a whole new book that was only based on *The Wizard of Oz*. They had ruby slippers instead of silver ones, there was only one good witch and it was all just a bad dream. Also, Dorothy was *much* older. I think I will keep on reading the Oz books. We chose the right time to read the book. I was just in a Purim play called *Follow the Hamatash Road*. I was a Winkie and I did the "Yo Hee Ho" march. It was fun!

Rachel Rosenthal

THE WIZARD OF OZ ESSAY

I have discovered that *The Wizard of Oz* is a stimulating vehicle for teaching the traditional essay. Often called a five-paragraph essay, this sort of expository writing is a mainstay of many middle and high schools. I have found that when children have something they are really interested in writing about, it becomes an interesting new form of writing for them to explore rather than a chore.

I always begin by modeling how to write such an essay. The students are much more used to writing creatively, so this is a new and difficult approach for them. They need lots of modeling and support to begin to succeed with it.

I read aloud Louis Sachar's *Holes* in 1999 shortly after it won the Newbery Award. My class loved it as much as I did. One thing I noted to them was that it seemed like a very masculine book, in other words, "a boy's book." Adults insisted to me that it wasn't because both girls and boys liked it, but it still seemed like one to me. So when it came time to model how to write an essay I knew I had my book and topic.

I began by demonstrating how I would plan out and then write a first draft of such an essay. (I recommend the planning sheets in the Writing Resource book from Heinemann's First Steps program. The following is based on their exposition-planning sheet.)

ESSAY PLAN

Problem and Point of View

Is it a "boy book" or a "girl book"? *Holes* is a boy's book.

Reasons and Specific Evidence

1. All main characters that you care about are boys

   - Evidence from the book:
     Stanley
     Zero

2. The style of the writing is masculine.

   - Evidence from the book:
     Nicknames
     Short sentence structure (use quote from page 4)
     Speaking style

3. Plot contains violence, gruesome, gory parts

   - Evidence from the book:
     Zero hits Mr. P with shovel
     Description of blisters
     Warden scratches face

SUMMARY/CONCLUSION

Restate main points above in different words.

The class and I then together began a first draft.

Gender and Louis Sachar's *Holes*

Holes is a realistic fiction novel by Louis Sachar. It's about a boy named Stanley who is sent to a juvenile center in Greenlake, Texas. He meets a lot of dirty, smelly, and interesting boys. Together they have to dig big holes even though they don't know why. The warden claims it builds character. Many people have debated if *Holes* is a "girl's book" or a "boy's book." Many members of the Edinger House feel it is more of a "boy's" book.

The main characters that you care about are boys. Stanley is the character that moves the story, along with his sidekick, Zero. There are very few females in the book and most of them are either mean or less important.

Another reason *Holes* seems more boy-like is....

In conclusion, *Holes* is mainly a boy's book even though girls might like reading it. The style of Holes is masculine, the plot contains gruesome parts and most of all, the main characters are boys.

After this exercise, students are ready to begin their own essays. First they create a class list of possible topics related to *The Wizard of Oz.*

- Is the MGM movie a good or bad adaptation of the book?

- Is Lewis Carroll a better writer than L. Frank Baum?

- Did Dorothy enjoy her adventures more than Alice?

- Which was better—the book or the movie?

- Where would you rather go: Wonderland or Oz?

- Compare Dorothy and Alice.

- Discuss one of the characters in the book.

After ample planning, drafting, and conferring each produces a final copy; see samples on the following pages.

FINAL THOUGHTS

The Wizard of Oz is the most American of literary fairy tales. Well known to us through the MGM film, it is a delightful story for children to explore in depth. Contrasting such a well-known film to the original book is an excellent way to develop students' analytic abilities. As new media becomes more and more prominent in our lives, it only makes sense to bring it into our teaching as well. Making connections between text and film is one way to do so. And there's no better way than with America's homegrown fairy tale: *The Wizard of Oz.*

The Wizard of Oz and
Alice's Adventures in Wonderland

An Essay By Marisa Kefalidis

The books The Wizard of Oz and Alice's Adventures in Wonderland are both about little girls going into made-up places. Dorothy is a girl from Kansas and Alice is from a wealthy family in England. The books are about their adventures in those places. I believe Alice is more independent, more adventurous, and more decisive.

I think Alice is more independent for many reasons. Alice stands up for herself a lot. Alice is always ready to show her side of the matter. For example, at the Tea Party and the courtroom, to the Caterpillar, to the mouse, and especially to the Queen. Dorothy has the Scarecrow, Cowardly Lion, Tin Woodman, and Toto as her companions. If Alice does not like something she stands up for herself or walks away. Dorothy would depend on a Cowardly Lion, Scarecrow, or anyone around her to do it for her. If the Scarecrow suggests an idea, Dorothy always says yes. Alice meets many people on her journey that she could have invited to join her on her journey. But she didn't. Those are the reasons I think Alice is more independent.

I think Alice is more adventurous for many reasons. Alice does not care as much about getting home. She just wants to go to the garden, but as you know, she deals with whatever happens. Alice does not mind if she gets sidetracked. She even played croquet with the mean Queen, she went to the Tea Party and was happy wherever she went. Alice might cry at times or make a wrong decision, but over all I think Alice is more adventurous. Dorothy just wants to go home. That is all she wants to do. As soon as she finds out that Oz can send her home she and Toto set off for Emerald City. She just follows the yellow brick road.

I think Alice is more decisive for many reasons. In the book Alice knows what her decisions are right away. Alice does not let anyone tell her what to do. Even the Cat. Alice does not want anyone bossing her around. Alice would much rather make as many decisions for herself as possible. No one in Wonderland would try to boss her around but the Queen. Dorothy can't get over the fact that she is not home yet so she has everyone and anyone make decisions for her. One example is when the Scarecrow says, "Why don't you call the Winged Monkeys?" and other things like that. I think she could have figured that out on her own.

In conclusion, I think Alice is more independent, adventurous, and more decisive than Dorothy.

Wizard of Oz Essay

By Nathaniel Shapiro

The Wizard of Oz has been a timeless classic in the eyes of both young and old for almost one hundred years. It is a story of a girl and a land of wonder, hence the name, "Wonderful Wizard of Oz." I will focus on a vital character in the book: the Tin Woodman, who, in this book, searches for a heart.

The Tin Woodman's worry about not having a heart begins with his feelings towards himself. He thinks (and literally believes) he is empty inside. He thinks less of himself because of his physical disadvantage of not having a heart. He thinks he can't love; he thinks he can't hate; he thinks he can't have feelings in general because he does not have a heart. He also thinks his appearance and what he is like are the same thing. Because he is made out of tin he believes he cannot have feelings.

Despite his feelings towards himself, the Tin Woodman's actions towards others prove that he truly has a heart. For instance, I believe he is very kind. If he did not have feelings, he would not have helped the mouse who was running away from the cat. If he did not have feelings he would not have any sadness or pity towards the mouse. If he had not felt friendship towards Dorothy and his other companions, he would not have killed the wolves that the Wicked Witch sent or chopped the log when the Kalidahs were chasing them. This proves that he is more loving than he thinks. It also proves that he thinks of others before himself which only someone with feelings would do.

In the end, the Tin Woodman learns many things about having a heart. He learns a heart isn't always something that is physical. Sometimes it is how you act. He also learns that he should be more self-confident. He learns that if he did not have a heart he would not have remorse about his misfortune.

I think the Tin Woodman teaches both Dorothy and the reader about what a heart really is. Having a heart is how you behave not how you are physically. I believe L. Frank Baum was trying to show the old proverb: it's what is on the inside that counts.

STUDENT PACKET

THE WIZARD OF OZ: Book into Film

INTRODUCTION

The Wizard of Oz is America's fairy tale. Many, many years ago, L. Frank Baum decided to write a modern fairy tale. He felt that traditional fairy tales like Cinderella were old-fashioned and that it was time for someone to write some new ones. So he wrote the ever-popular Oz stories. Today we know them best because of the 1939 MGM movie. Judy Garland as Dorothy, the ruby slippers, and "Over the Rainbow" are what we think of when we think of Oz.

We will begin by reading L. Frank Baum's The Wizard of Oz. After our initial reading, we will investigate Baum and consider how and why he wrote the Oz books. In our roles as literary scholars, we will also compare The Wizard of Oz to other well-known fantasies such as Alice in Wonderland. Next we will view the 1939 movie, examine its creation, and compare it to the original book. By the end of the unit, you should all be Oz-experts!

L. FRANK BAUM

L. Frank Baum was born in Chittenango, New York in 1856. He worked as a salesman, a playwright, and a journalist before becoming a writer of children's books. His first great success was *Father Goose, His Book*, a collection of poems illustrated by W. W. Denslow. *The Wizard of Oz*, with illustrations by Denslow, was published in 1900. It was a tremendous success right away. Eventually, many other Oz books were also written, but *The Wizard of Oz* has always been the most well known.

Baum had been thinking about writing a fairy tale for some time. The Oz stories began as bedtime stories for his children and their friends which Baum then wrote into an early draft titled *The Emerald City*. His publishers disliked the title because they were fearful that a book with a jewel in the title wouldn't sell. Other titles under consideration were *From Kansas to Fairyland*, *The Fairyland of Oz*, and *The Land of Oz*.

The *Wizard of Oz* came out in 1900, two years after Lewis Carroll's death. While *The Wizard of Oz* is quite different from *Alice in Wonderland*, they are often compared. It seems likely that Baum was familiar with Carroll's work and was trying to create his own imaginary land with a girl heroine.

Baum wrote 13 more Oz books as well as stage versions of the stories. He died at Ozcot, his Hollywood home, on May 6, 1919.

MEMORIES OF *THE WIZARD OF OZ*

Some of you may already know something about the story. If you have had some experience with the story, please write about it below. You may have seen a movie version, read the book, had it read to you, or performed in a camp version of the story.

_____

_____

_____

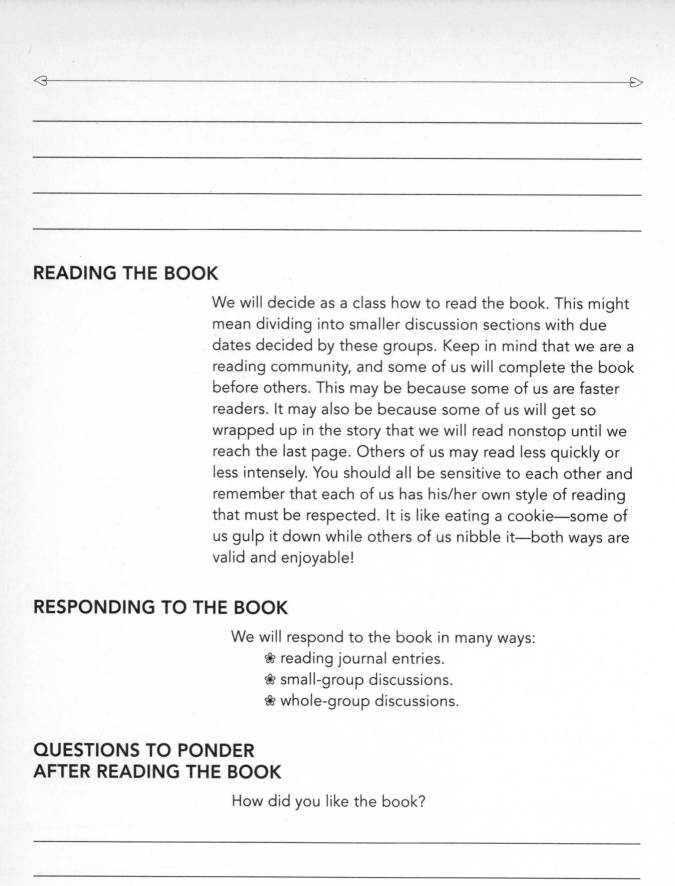

_____

_____

_____

_____

READING THE BOOK

We will decide as a class how to read the book. This might mean dividing into smaller discussion sections with due dates decided by these groups. Keep in mind that we are a reading community, and some of us will complete the book before others. This may be because some of us are faster readers. It may also be because some of us will get so wrapped up in the story that we will read nonstop until we reach the last page. Others of us may read less quickly or less intensely. You should all be sensitive to each other and remember that each of us has his/her own style of reading that must be respected. It is like eating a cookie—some of us gulp it down while others of us nibble it—both ways are valid and enjoyable!

RESPONDING TO THE BOOK

We will respond to the book in many ways:
* reading journal entries.
* small-group discussions.
* whole-group discussions.

QUESTIONS TO PONDER
AFTER READING THE BOOK

How did you like the book?

_____

_____

_____

Who was your favorite character? Why?

_____

_____

_____

_____

_____

Do you note any similarities to and/or differences from other books you have read?

_____

_____

_____

_____

_____

_____

THE METRO-GOLDWYN-MAYER MOVIE

While there were several earlier Oz movies, the 1939 MGM one is the most well known. No expense was spared in making this movie. A great search was made for the perfect Dorothy; even the highly popular Shirley Temple was considered for the role. Eventually 16-year-old Judy Garland was selected even though Dorothy is described in the book as a much younger child.

The movie story is quite different from the book. Whole chapters were left out and, most notably, Oz becomes Dorothy's dream. The result is a very different story from Baum's.

QUESTIONS TO PONDER AFTER VIEWING THE MGM MOVIE

How did you like the movie?

_____

_____

_____

_____

_____

_____

Who was your favorite character in the movie? Was it the same as your favorite character in the book?

_____

_____

_____

_____

_____

_____

_____

Using Beloved Classics to Deepen Reading Comprehension • Scholastic Professional Books

How did it compare to the book?

_____

_____

_____

_____

_____

_____

_____

_____

_____

_____

_____

_____

Using Beloved Classics to Deepen Reading Comprehension • Scholastic Professional Books

Digging Deep with Reading Aloud

"What about a story?" said Christopher Robin.
"What about a story?" I said.

—A. A. MILNE
WINNIE-THE-POOH

A typical day in my classroom: Writing workshop has just ended. Students are busy, putting away folders, tying shoes, going out for drinks, admiring someone's new eraser. There is the sound of productive bustle; these kids know exactly what they are doing. Before long someone has turned out the light. Now students are getting pillows and stretching out on the rug. One takes her special place under my desk; others stay at their own desks, some in seats, others sprawled on top. A few sit as close to me as possible, at my feet, leaning against my chair, or sitting on my desk. Soon it is quiet. I open the book. Story time has begun.

I have always loved being read to. There was my father, sitting by my bed, reading the vain attempts of a cat to half talk in Edgar Eager's *Half Magic*. Or my prim sixth-grade teacher, facing us in our rows, as she read the next chapter of *Born to Trot*. I could have read those books on my own, of course, but there was something different and special about having them read to me. Recently, at a restaurant, a good friend spent most of the meal regaling me with his favorite parts of Dave Barry's latest book. I may read the book on my own at some point, but listening to my friend so gleefully reading was an equally pleasurable experience. However old we are, listening to someone read is always delightful. And while all kinds of written material can and should be read aloud in classrooms, fantasy literature, which began in the words of storytellers and the oral tradition, is a particularly suitable vehicle for story time.

DIGGING DEEP WITH READ-ALOUDS

 he longer I teach the more I see how important reading aloud is. Too often reading aloud is seen by educators as something for primary-aged children, that older children should be reading on their own. However, more and more teachers of upper elementary and middle school students are carving out time in their busy days to read aloud to their students as well. Story time has been a part of my day as a teacher ever since I began teaching years ago. For many years it was a special time devoted to novels. I looked for exciting books, books that made my students beg me not to stop, books that helped my reluctant readers take pleasure in literature, books that provoked conversation. I selected books that encouraged deep thinking as well as those that were simply fun and and entertaining. More recently, while keeping my

special daily story time, I've begun reading aloud more and more at other times of the day as well. Poetry now often begins or ends our day. Wonderful works of nonfiction enhance our history studies. Picture books enchant at any time. Reading aloud, I've discovered, can enhance students' learning and provoke deep thinking all day long.

STORY TIME

While I now read aloud throughout the day, my favorite time continues to be story time. It is usually in the afternoon when my students are a bit overstimulated and need time to quiet down and relax. I've scheduled it after recess, after gym, and right before dismissal. Whenever it is scheduled, the rituals are always the same. I developed them many years ago and they have remained remarkably constant. Out go the overhead lights and on goes my small reading lamp.

I settle into my special reading chair and wait for my students to make themselves comfortable. Once all is ready we begin. I generally read for 20 minutes, usually one chapter. Students love it when I leave off at an especially exciting point. It makes them anxious, of course, for story time the next day. Our ritual becomes so important to my students that they detest any variation. For example, they hate having the light on, even if it means not seeing illustrations well. Time after time they've told me that they prefer to create their own images in their minds as they listen. As a result I rarely show illustrations unless they are integral to the story. Other teachers have other rituals. Some light special candles to set the mood. Others play music. Still others have special chants to begin and end the story time. Whatever works best for you, the teacher, is what I recommend.

BOOKS FOR STORY TIME

ook selection for story time needs to be a balance of teacher input and student suggestions. Sometimes I present more than one book to my class and ask them to vote. If I begin a book and sense that the class is not enjoying it, I will ask for another vote. I see no point plugging on with a read-aloud selection if the audience has lost interest. Books that work for one class may not work for another.

I select books that I like, that read aloud well, and that correspond to the interests of the particular group of students I have at a given time. While I enjoy fantasy literature and read aloud a lot of it, I also read aloud other kinds of literature. My students are usually big fans of animal stories. For many years, my first book was always Phyllis Reynolds Naylor's *The Grand Escape,* a delightful animal fantasy. Realistic fiction is also worthwhile. I've put my students in stitches with Gary Paulsen's fictional memoir, *Harris and Me.* Another favorite of mine and my students, a realistic novel that reads like a tall tale, is Jerry Spinelli's *Maniac Magee.* All of these books have the kind of strong narrative voices that make them especially good as read-alouds.

Some points to consider when selecting a novel to read aloud:

1. An exciting narrative is important. I read aloud for about 15 to 20 minutes, and I can usually read a chapter in that time. Leaving my audience in suspense until the next day is a great part of reading aloud. It makes my students anticipate with delight the next day's reading. My students groaned when I ended a chapter of Gail Carson Levine's *Dave at Night,* so eager were they to know what would happen next.

2. Interesting characters that students can relate to are important. Maniac Magee is one, as is Dave. If the characters are animals, or imaginary characters like dragons, they still need to have human traits that students can enjoy. Roald Dahl's books are full of such characters.

3. Well-developed dialogue is important. The reader can read different characters as different voices. Too much description can bore a young audience.

4. Students who are not good listeners can be won over with humor. My first book of the year is usually a humorous one.

READING ALOUD NONFICTION

More and more I read aloud nonfiction to my students. Poetry has often been a way we start or end the day. Sometimes I select and read the poems, while sometimes my students do so. I've also read aloud many interesting books to enrich our history studies. Sometimes they are works of historical fiction (say, an imaginary diary of a *Mayflower* passenger). Sometimes they are photobiographies. And sometimes they are actually documents and journals from long ago times.

READING ALOUD PICTURE BOOKS

There are many wonderful picture books that are perfect for middle and upper elementary students. I often read such books during our morning meetings. They are short and often provoke wonderful discussions. Teachers underestimate the power of picture books to stimulate deep thinking about literature.

Many teachers begin the year with a special book. For the last few years my book for this purpose has been *Hurray for Diffendorfer Day*. This is a book that was left unfinished by Dr. Seuss. Jack Prelutsky finished the text and Lane Smith finished the illustrations. The final book is a delightful homage to Dr. Seuss and individualization as well. My students delight in picking out the many familiar Seuss characters scattered throughout Smith's illustrations. Additionally, they are fascinated by the information provided by the editor, Janet Schulman, as to how the book came to be.

Other picture books that intrigue my students are Jon Scieczka and Lane Smith's *Math Curse,* and Chris Raschka's *Mysterious Thelonious.*

RESPONDING TO READ-ALOUDS

y students have responded to the stories I read aloud in many different ways. Most common is the simple, contented silence that happens when I close the book at the end of a session, the sort of happy silence that means they have truly enjoyed the reading. Sometimes we talk a bit further about the story so far, and other times we leave it for ourselves to think about alone. I don't feel any need to quiz my students on their understanding of the story. I trust they understand it, and I know if they don't, they will ask for clarification. My main point in story time is having my students learn to take pleasure in literature, not to check their listening skills.

Certain books demand more. When I read a novel that is especially mysterious, we often discuss what we think will happen next. Sometimes we discuss how the book is like others we know or what we like and don't like about it. Occasionally the read-aloud book does indeed relate to our

other studies. For example, I began reading aloud *The Orphan of Ellis Island* right after we returned from our field trip to the actual island. Students enjoyed discussing the author's description of the museum and how the immigration experiences described in the book compared to what they were learning.

I have found that asking students to write in their response journals is a good way to extend the story time. I always invite my students to respond to the read-aloud in their journals. Occasionally, if I want to get a more detailed sense of how they feel about a particular book, I might assign them a response to the book. Here are some responses to *The Boggart* by Susan Cooper.

I really think that The Boggart is a really good read aloud. When you were first reading the book to us I didn't think the book was all that great but then one day I started to really enjoy it. Today when you stopped I'm really just in suspense.

Anne Kurtz

I like The Boggart because of all the tricks that the Boggart plays. Also, I think the book is written well. You can see what is happening. Can the Boggart talk? The author never did make the Boggart say anything so far. I think in the end, the Boggart will go back to the castle.

Eric Kiung

On several occasions books I've read aloud lent themselves to letter writing. In 1997 I came across Gail Carson Levine's delightful retelling of the Cinderella story, *Ella*

Enchanted. My students so enjoyed this book that we ended up writing a class letter to Gail. She responded with pleasure, offering to come visit the class. Shortly thereafter we were delighted when the book was named a Newbery Honor book. Last year I read aloud Levine's book, *Dave at Night.* I thought students would enjoy it because it took place in many parts of New York that they knew. While I read it during our *Cinderella* unit I did not see it as having any connections to that unit. However, I went to a talk by Gail Carson Levine where she spoke of how she wrote *Dave at Night.* As I listened I realized that the book had numerous *Cinderella* elements and might indeed be a Cinderella story. I pointed some of these out to Gail after her talk, but she seemed rather dubious. Returning to my class I asked them what they thought. They were adamant. *Dave at Night* WAS a Cinderella story in their opinions. I asked them if they were interested in writing Gail and telling her so. They were thrilled and here are excerpts from Jane, Elizabeth, and Isabelle's letters along with an excerpt from Gail's letter back to the class.

Dear Ms. Levine,

I have to say *Dave at Night* was one of the best books I have ever been read to! It really kept me interested. I liked the book so much that I might read it by myself!

My class is doing a study of Cinderella. I find it very interesting. We have been reading lots and lots of variants of Cinderella. Sometimes when we read a book that is not meant to be a Cinderella we find elements in that book that related to Cinderella.

I think *Dave at Night* is like a Cinderella because, first of all, both his parents die. He has a magical helper, Solly...It has a big event, not a ball, but getting back Papa's carving. And

also there is an element in this book that sort of connects to Cinderella. It is that Dave lost his shoe.

Jane Meyerson

Dear Ms. Levine,

Dave at Night really interacted with our studies here at Dalton. I know Ms. Edinger is trying to convince you that *Dave at Night* is a Cindy story. Although I don't know you (and believe me I want to meet you) I am on Ms. Edinger's side.

I think *Dave at Night* is a Cindy story because it fits like a puzzle. It has all of the pieces. Solly is the magical helper because he pulls Dave out of the HHB and brings food and is nice to him. And then there are the roles of the stepmother as played by Mr. Doom, the role of the stepsister is Moe because he is mean and steals food. And Ida is also a stepmother because she gives him away to the HHB and is also mean. The "ball" Dave is trying to get to is Irma Lee's party. Now, have Ms. Edinger and I convinced you?

Elizabeth Sacks

Dear Ms. Levine,

I strongly believe that *Dave at Night* is a Cinderella story. Because, I mean think, Solly could be the fairy godfather. Irma Lee's birthday party could be the ball. Dave's parents die. There are many people who are mean to him and, most of all, he loses his shoe on the run to Aunt Sarah and Aunt Lily.

Isabelle Glimcher

Dear Ms. Edinger's Class,

Thank you so much for your wonderful letters, and I'm delighted that you enjoyed *Dave at Night*. You've convinced me that it is a Cinderella story. I had no idea of the connection when I had Dave lose his shoe. I just wanted his foot to get wet on his way downtown—part of any author's responsibility to make his or her characters as miserable as possible!

Here's something else to think about—although both Dave and Ella are Cinderella stories, Cinderella isn't the plot of either one. The plot of both books is a quest. In Ella the quest is a way to end the curse. In Dave the quest is for his carving and for a home once he gets the carving back. The Cinderella elements are embellishments, add-ons. What do you think? Do you agree?

Gail C. Levine

The final proof of what my students had discovered came during the summer of 2000. In Inside Borders, the Borders Bookstore newsletter, was Gail's article, "Bringing Fairy Tales Up to Speed." In it she wrote, "My *Dave at Night* (HarperCollins, 1999) is a historical novel, definitely not a fairy tale—or so I thought till a fourth grade class convinced me otherwise. They sent me letters, insisting that Dave is Cinderella all over again. They pointed out that he has an evil stepmother and a helper who plays the part of the fairy godfather. The clincher came when they reminded me that Dave loses one shoe (representing the glass slipper) at the story's climax. I had no idea when I wrote the book!"

CHOOSING BOOKS FOR READ-ALOUDS

Generally the special read-aloud time in my classroom is devoted to a novel. I want to excite students about books and reading and look for books that will stimulate them in many ways. For example, I look for books that leave students hanging, anxiously awaiting the next day's reading. I also enjoy reading aloud books that encourage my more reluctant readers to return to the book on their own or to explore another book by the same author.

EXPRESSIVE READINGS

There is certainly a skill in reading aloud. My students love different voices for different characters, a raise in my voice and a quickening in tempo at a particularly exciting part of the story. Consider reading aloud as a performance. Just as you are performing when you are teaching a lesson, so you are when you are reading aloud. You need to make it exciting, scary, funny—whatever the book calls for. It is the reader's responsibility to the text, to the author, and to the audience to keep the book alive through his or her performance.

FINAL THOUGHTS

Reading aloud is as much fun for me as for my students. Our story time is probably the time of the day where we are closest. Students complain if we miss a single session of this very important time. I am sure too that it is another wonderful way to help students dig deep into literature. The books I read intrigue them, sometimes enough to find others by the same authors. Elements in the stories surprise us in all kinds of ways. There are no heavy-handed expectations for my students during our read-aloud times (other than those of etiquette). We simply are a group of people all enjoying a book together. What could be more fun than that?

Digging Deep with Independent Reading

"And when the firemen turned off the hose and were standing in the wet, smoky room, Jim's aunt, Miss Prothero, came downstairs and peered in at them. Jim and I waited very quietly, to hear what she would say to them. She said the right thing always. She looked at the three tall firemen in their shiny helmets, standing among the smoke and cinders and dissolving snowballs, and she said: Would you like anything to read?"

—DYLAN THOMAS
*A CHILD'S CHRISTMAS
IN WALES*

I'm a New Yorker, which means I occasionally take the subway. Due to a propensity towards carsickness I can't read. However, most of my fellow passengers do read, no matter how crowded, hot, dirty, or noisy the train is. The diversity of reading material is remarkable. I see thrillers, classics, magazines, textbooks, memos, newsletters, romances, and mysteries. I love looking over someone's shoulder at a Russian newspaper, trying to figure out the headlines. Tourists seriously study guidebooks as they scramble out to view the sights. How great to live in a city of readers!

I want my students to be lifelong readers, to read for enjoyment and pleasure, not merely to pass a test or to get the latest stock report. I want them to be the kind of people who take lots of books on vacation, who enjoy browsing in a bookstore, who read on public transportation. To develop such a temperment, students must not only read a lot, but also have plenty of opportunities to select their own reading material. Just as students are individuals, their book choices are highly personal. Some students lean toward sports stories while others adore realistic animal sagas. Some are series aficionados, still others prefer informational texts. And finally, there are the fantasy buffs, lovers of other worlds and magical beings.

DIGGING DEEP INTO LITERATURE THROUGH INDEPENDENT READING

As much as I love overseeing an author study or reading aloud a particularly wonderful book, I consider developing enthusiastic independent readers one of the most important things I do as a teacher. Many of my students come into fourth grade most reluctant about reading. They often become excited as we study *Charlotte's Web*, *Cinderella*, and *Alice's Adventures in Wonderland*. However, it is when they become excited about the books they select and read on their own that I become excited as well.

STRUCTURING INDEPENDENT READING

From the first day of school, I make it very clear that the most important homework expected for my class is the half hour of nightly reading. This is not considered something to do in addition to regular homework—it *is* "regular

homework." Parents and I work together with children, helping them find books they like, a good place to read, a way to plan reading. At first, reluctant readers need lots of help with this assignment. But I have found that with parent support most of my fourth-graders become far more comfortable with the assignment as the year goes on.

I keep track of students' independent reading via individual conferences, journal entries, and group discussions. I must admit that I struggle to find time to see my students often for individual conferences. With all the other work going on, these reading conferences are not as frequent as I would like. My students and I enjoy a few minutes chatting about a book. I always ask students to tell me what they are reading, how they like it, what they plan to read next, if they want any help from me.

Most of my interaction with my students and their independent reading centers around their journals. I schedule a weekly journal time. We talk about possible journal entries. I sometimes ask students to read favorite journal entries to the group, and then the students use the remainder of the time to write their entries. If entries are too brief I set a time requirement: They must write for ten minutes, for example. I feel a time requirement works much better than word- or page-length. If students know they must write for a certain amount of time they usually begin thinking of something to write about.

JOURNAL RESPONSES TO INDEPENDENT READING

As the year goes on and my students become more adept at making literary connections, they enjoy finding ties between independent reading and group literature books. The following journal excerpts demonstrate the different ways my students select books, read at home, and respond to their reading.

I just finished reading *James and the Giant Peach* for the tenth time, but it's still one of my favorites. Now I've read all of Dahl's children's books except *The Twits*, but I plan on reading it as soon as possible. I hear it's really funny. I seem to have a strange habit of always eating a peach whenever I read it!

Rachel Rosenthal

I really like the *Half Magic* series even though I'm not done with it. So far I've read four of the books. I like the *Half Magic* series because the books just take me to another land. It's as if I'm the person that the adventure is happening to. What I really like that occurs in all of Edgar Eager's books is that you know as much as the characters know. I mean, he doesn't tell you things the characters don't know. All I know is that I really like his books.

Sarah Wertheimer

At home I'm reading *The Lion, The Witch, and the Wardrobe.* I read it last year, but I wanted to read it again because my mom gave it to me, it was fourth grade level, so I thought I might want to read it again, because I might not have understood all of it. . .*The Lion, the Witch, and the Wardrobe* is very serious. It has nothing funny. It is sort of like *Cinderella* because at first the four kids in the beginning were just regular kids. Then in the end the kids become kings and queens. The book seems to go by very slow. In *The Wizard of Oz* the book goes by very fast and you enjoy it a lot more too because it has a story with a lot of action...

Richard Zbeda

I'm reading *A Wrinkle in Time.* I started on Monday. The first time I saw the book I thought it was going to be about aliens. I think I know why, because the cover is a little weird. But then as it came to a surprise to me that it had normal people and that they lived in a normal house and they went to a normal school. I think the way the author started the book was interesting. What I thought was a sort of good way to start off the book was that they couldn't find their father. One of my favorite characters is Charles Wallace because he always knows how Meg is feeling and what she wants. Something that I feel is not good about Meg is that when she gets mad or frustrated is that she blames it on somebody and gets into a fight.

Anne Kurtz

I'm reading *The B.F.G.* and I really like it because it is funny and I've never heard of a Big Friendly Giant. I read it to Sean and Erin, my sisters, and they liked it because one of the main characters in the book is Sophie and I have a cousin named Sophie. They also liked the idea of a Big Friendly Giant and I like it when he's catching dreams the most.

I'm not all the way done but close.

Mack Cauley

I am reading *Dealing With Dragons.* My favorite characters in the book are the dragons. I think it is because it is interesting how human like they are. I like it because it is funny and the wizards are dumb. I like this kind of book. There is a guy who is minding his own business, but then he either wants to or does something spectacular. Like *The*

Trumpet of the Swan. Louis is dumb and wants to speak (or trumpet). His journey takes place because he has to repay the trumpet his father stole.

Eric Kiung

INFORMAL CONVERSATIONS ABOUT INDEPENDENT READING

ne of my favorite way to interact with my students about their independent reading is through informal conversations. These differ from reading conferences in that they tend to be before school starts, during lunch and recess, or after school. While reading conferences are one on one, these informal conversations can involve a small group of students who all want to talk about a particular book. Sometimes it is a book that has been making its way through my class, one student after another reading it. Or sometimes it is a book that many have read and would like to discuss again and again. I love these conversations because they are generated by students and are the most authentic of any of our classroom conversations about books. In these conversations, my students express their greatest enthusiasm for reading. Those overhearing such conversations join in and often decide to read a book after listening to us talk about it with such enthusiasm.

J. K. Rowling's Harry Potter books, I've discovered, are especially good at provoking such informal conversations. While many teachers have read these books aloud to their classes, I prefer to have children read them as independent reading books. This is because they are quite long and I prefer to read shorter books aloud. (So that if there is a student in the class who doesn't like the book, he or she doesn't have to suffer it too long.) I also have discovered that students who like the Harry Potter books are motivated to read them on their own. They don't need to be nudged into reading them. Some teachers read them aloud because the students they teach can not yet read them independently. However, I feel they are such fun books for independent reading that students should wait until they are at a reading level where they can read them independently.

I first came across the Harry Potter books while visiting England in August of 1998. I saw the second book on display all over the place, but ignored it thinking it was some sort of mystery like the Hardy Boys. However, upon returning to the United States I read a brief review of *Harry Potter and the Sorcerer's Stone* and, intrigued, immediately bought the book. I enjoyed it and gave it to first one and then other students in my class. As the book was passed around, the children who read it enjoyed discussing it informally. We all wondered what the next book would be like and were delighted to get a copy from a parent who travelled to England. The following year more of my students had read the first two books and were beginning to read the third. I had to encourage a few children to suspend reading the book as it was evident to me they were reading it only because it was popular, not because they liked it at all. However, we the Harry Potter enthusiasts had a grand time discussing the different characters and what we thought would happen in the next book.

The reason these informal book talks happen, I believe, is that my students know how much I love literature. They look to me for book recommendations and then want to discuss the books once they have read them. While they enjoy our correspondence in their response journals, they enjoy these informal talks as well. My recommendation is to read as many popular children's books as possible and to demonstrate how much you truly like them to your students through informal book talks.

Final Thoughts

While this may be the shortest chapter in this book, the idea behind it is probably the most significant: the importance of independent reading. Fourth-graders, I've discovered, are often just moving from learning to read to enjoying reading. In addition to exciting them about literature through our deep literary studies and my read alouds, I also want to excite them about reading on their own. I encourage them to discover for themselves which books they like so that they end up wanting to read through meals and past bedtime. I can't say that every student in my classes finishes the year with this sort of view of reading, but certainly many more finish the year with this attitude then start it.

With the greater and greater attraction of the Internet, video games, and other non-book activities, we are finding people (children and adults) who *can* read, but choose to do so rarely. My hope is to encourage young people to see the pleasure that the quiet reading of a work of literature can provide, to help them discover that they can dig deep into a great book all by themselves.

Bibliography

Note: All websites were current at time of publication. However, addresses may have changed since publication.

CHAPTER 1
BOOKS AND ARTICLES

Atwell, Nancie. (1998). *In the Middle*. Portsmouth, NH: Heinemann.

Ellis, Sarah. (2000). *From Reader to Writer: Teaching Writing through Classic Children's Books*. Toronto, Canada: Groundwood Books.

Buzzeo, Toni and Jane Kurtz. (1999). *Terrific Connections with Authors, Illustrators, and Storytellers: Real Space and Virtual Links*. Englewood, CO: Libraries Unlimited.

Graves, Donald. (1991). *Build a Literate Classroom*. Portsmouth, NH: Heinemann.

Harwayne, Shelley. (1991). *Lasting Impressions: Weaving Literature into the Writing Workshop*. Portsmouth, NH: Heinemann.

Horning, Kathleen T. (1997*). From Cover to Cover: Evaluating and Reviewing Children's Books*. New York: HarperCollins.

Kiefer, Barbara Z. (1995*). The Potential of Picturebooks: From Visual Literacy to Aesthetic Understanding*. Englewood Cliffs, NJ: Prentice Hall.

Moss, Joy F. (1990). *Focus on Literature: A Context for Literacy Learning*. Katonah, NY: Richard C. Owens.

Nodelman, Perry. (1996). *The Pleasures of Children's Literature*. New York: Longman.

Pennac, Daniel. (1999). *Better Than Life*. York, Maine: Stenhouse.

Peterson, Ralph and Maryann Eeds. (1990). *Grand Conversations: Literature Groups in Action*. Toronto, Canada: Scholastic.

Ray, Katie Wood. (1999). *Wondrous Words: Writers and Writing in the Elementary School*. Urbana, IL: National Council of Teachers of English.

Rosenblatt, Louise M. (1991). "Literature—S.O.S." *Language Arts*, 68.

Rosenblatt, Louise M. (1983). *Literature as Exploration*. New York: Modern Language Association.

Silvey, Anita, Ed. (1995). *Children's Books and Their Creators*. Boston, MA: Houghton Mifflin.

Sloan, Glenna Davis. (1991). *The Child as Critic: Teaching Literature in Elementary and Middle Schools*. New York: Teachers College Press.

PROFESSIONAL JOURNALS

The following are a selection of journals that offer reviews of children's books. Each has both a print and online edition. For each I have given the online address where additional information on both the online and print editions is available.

Book Links
http://www.ala.org/BookLinks/008.html

Book List
http://www.ala.org/booklist

The Bulletin of the Center for Children's Books
http://www.lis.uiuc.edu/puboff/bccb

The Horn Book
http://www.hbook.com/mag.shtml

Riverbank Review
http://www.riverbankreview.com

School Library Journal
http://www.slj.com

WEB SITES

The Children's Literature Web Guide
http://www.acs.ucalgary.ca/~dkbrown/index.html

Carol Hurst's Children's Literature Web Site
http://www.carolhurst.com

CHAPTER 2

BOOKS

Elledge, Scott. (1984). *E.B. White: A Biography*. New York: W.W. Norton and Company.

Gherman, Beverly. (1992). *E.B. White: Some Writer!* New York: Atheneum.

White, E. B. (1994). *The Annotated Charlotte's Web*. Illustrated by Garth Williams. Introduction and Notes by Peter F. Neumeyer. New York: HarperCollins.

WEB SITES

E. B. White
http://www.harperchildrens.com/hch/author/author/white

CHAPTER 3

PICTURE BOOK CINDERELLAS

Brown, Marcia. (1954). *Cinderella*. New York: Macmillan.

Cinderella. Facsimile of 1859 shape book. Chester, CT: Applewood Books.

Climo, Shirley. (1989). *The Egyptian Cinderella*. Illustrated by Ruth Heller. New York: Crowell.

————. (1993). *The Korean Cinderella*. Illustrated by Ruth Heller. New York: HarperCollins.

————. (1996). *The Irish Cinderlad*. Illustrated by Loretta Kruminski. New York: HarperCollins.

————. (1999). *The Persian Cinderella*. Illustrated by Robert Florczak. New York: HarperCollins.

Cole, Babette. (1987). *Prince Cinders*. New York: Sandcastle Books.

Compton, Joanne. (1994). *Ashpet*. Illustrated by Kenn Compton. New York: Holiday House.

Delamare, David. (1993). *Cinderella*. New York: Green Tiger Press.

Dijs, Carla. (1991). *Cinderella*. New York: Dell Yearling.

Easton, Samantha. (1992). *Cinderella*. Illustrated by Lynn Bywater. Kansas City: Andrews and McMeel.

Edwards, Pamela Duncan. (1997). *Dinorella*. Illustrated by Henry Cole. New York: Hyperion.

Erlich, Amy. (1985). *Cinderella*. Illustrated by Susan Jeffers. New York: Dial.

Evans, C.S. (1987). *Cinderella*. Illustrated by Arthur Rackham. London: Chancellor Press.

Hayes, Joe. (2000). *Estrellita de Oro: Little Golden Star*. Illustrated by Gloria Osuna Perez and Lucia Angela Perez. El Paso, TX: Cinco Puntos Press.

Hickox, Rebecca. (1998). *The Golden Sandal: A Middle Eastern Cinderella Story*. Illustrated by Will Hillenbrand. New York: Holiday House.

Hooks, William H. (1987). *Moss Gown*. Illustrated by Donald Carrick. New York: Clarion Books.

Huck, Charlotte. (1989). *Princess Furball*. Illustrated by Anita Lobel. New York: Greenwillow.

Jackson, Ellen. (1994). *Cinder Edna*. Illustrated by Kevin O'Malley. Lothrop, Lee & Shepard: New York.

Jaffe, Nina. (1998). *The Way Meat Loves Salt*. Illustrated by Louise August. New York: Henry Holt.

Karlin, Barbara. (1989). *Cinderella*. Illustrated by James Marshall. New York: Little Brown.

Ketteman, Helen. (1997). *Bubba the Cowboy Prince: A Fractured Texas Tale*. Illustrated by James Warhola. New York: Scholastic.

Levine, Gail Carson. (1997). *Ella Enchanted*. New York: HarperTrophy.

Louie, Ai-Ling. *(1982.)* Illustrated by Ed Young. *Yeh-Shen*. New York: Philomel.

Lowell, Susan. (2000). *Cindy Ellen: A Wild West Cinderella*. Illustrated by Jaen Manning. New York: HarperCollins.

Martin, Rafe. (1992). *The Rough-Face Girl*. Illustrated by David Shannon. New York: G.P. Putnam's Sons.

Minters, Frances. (1994). *Cinder-Elly*. Illustrated by G. Brian Karas. New York: Viking.

Myers, Bernice. (1985). *Sidney Rella and the Glass Sneaker.* New York: Macmillan.

Perlman, Janet. (1992). *Cinderella Penguin or The Little Glass Flipper.* Toronto: Kids Can Press.

Perrault, Charles. (1972). *Cinderella or the Little Glass Slipper.* Illustrated by Errol Le Cain. New York: Viking Penguin.

Pienkowski, Jan. (1977). *Cinderella.* New York: Alfred A. Knopf.

San Jose, Christine. (1994). *Cinderella.* Illustrated by Deborah Santini. Honesdale, PA: Boyds Mills Press.

San Souci, Robert D. (1994). *The Talking Eggs.* Illustrated by Jerry Pinkney. New York: Ballantine.

———. (1994). *Sootface.* Illustrated by Daniel San Souci. New York: Doubleday.

———. (1998). *Cendrillon: A Carribbean Cinderella.* Illustrated by Brian Pinkney. New York: Simon & Schuster.

Shorto, Russell. (1990). *Cinderella.* Illustrated by T. Lewis. New York: Birch Lane.

Steptoe, John. (1987). *Mufaro's Beautiful Daughters.* New York: Lothrop, Lee & Shepard Books.

Storey, Rita. (1992). *Cinderella.* Illustrated by Amelia Rosato. London: Puffin Books.

Walt Disney's Moving Picture Flip Book. B. Shackman and Co.

Wegman, William. (1993). *Cinderella.* New York: Hyperion.

Wilson, Barbara Ker. *Wishbones.* (1993). Illustrated by Meilo So. New York: Bradbury.

Winthrop, Elizabeth. (1991). *Vasilissa the Beautiful.* Illustrated by Alexander Koshkin. New York: HarperCollins.

Yorink, Arthur. (1990). *Ugh.* Illustrated by Richard Egielski. New York: Farrar Straus Giroux.

CINDERELLAS IN COLLECTIONS

Ahlberg, Janet and Allan. (1986). Cinderella. In *The Jolly Postman.* Boston: Little Brown.

Brooke, William J. (1990). The Fitting of the Slipper. In *A Telling of Tales.* New York: Harper and Row.

Brothers Grimm. (1987). "Cinderella." In *The Complete Fairy Tales of the Brothers Grimm*. Translated by Jack Zipes. New York: Bantam.

Carter, Angela. (1981). Cinderella: or, The Little Glass Slipper. In *Sleeping Beauty and Other Favorite Fairy Tales*. Illustrated by Michael Foreman. Boston: Joshua Morris.

Chase, Richard. (1976). "Ashpet." In *Grandfather Tales*. Boston: Houghton Mifflin.

Dahl, Roald. Cinderella. (1988). In *Revolting Rhymes*. Illustrated by Quentin Blake. New York: Bantam.

Edens, Cooper. (1991). Cinderella. In *The Three Princesses: Cinderella, Sleeping Beauty, Snow White: The Ultimate Illustrated Edition*. New York: Bantam Books.

Garner, James Finn. (1994). Cinderella. In *Politically Correct Bedtime Stories*. New York. Macmillan.

Lardner, Ring. (1926) Cinderella. In *What Of It?* New York: Scribner's.

Perrault, Charles. (1974). Cinderella. In *The Classic Fairy Tales*. Eds. Iona and Peter Opie. New York: Oxford University Press.

Perrault, Charles. (1969). "Cinderella or The Little Glass Slipper." Translated by A. E. Johnson. New York: Dover.

Perrault, Charles. (1991). Cinderella. In *The Sleeping Beauty and Other Classic French Fairy Tales*. Illustrated by W. Heath Robinson. New York: Children's Classics.

Scieszka, Jon. (1992). Cinderumpelstiltskin. In *The Stinky Cheese Man and Other Fairly Stupid Fairy Tales*. Illustrated by Lane Smith. New York: Viking.

Sexton, Anne. (1971). Cinderella. In *Transformations*. Boston: Houghton Mifflin.

Viorst, Judith. ...And Then the Prince Knelt Down and Tried to Put the Glass Slipper on Cinderella's Foot. (1987). In *Don't Bet on the Prince: Contemporary Feminist Fairy Tales in North America and England*. New York: Routledge.

BOOK-LENGTH CINDERELLAS

Haddix, Margret Peterson. (1999). *Just Ella*. New York: Simon & Schuster.

Levine, Gail Carson. (1997). *Ella Enchanted*. New York: HarperCollins.

Levine, Gail Carson. (2000). *Cinderellis and the Glass Hill*. New York: HarperCollins.

Pullman, Philip. Illustrated by Kevin Hawkes. (2000). *I Was a Rat!* New York: Knopf.

Mah, Adeline Yen. (1999). *Chinese Cinderella*. New York: Delecorte Press.

CINDERELLA MOVIES

There are many Cinderella videos available. I've got a Muppet version, one on ice, and numerous ballet versions. However, I don't particularly like them all. I am selective about the ones I show in class and the following are all videos I've found work successfully with my students. Most of these are available for purchase either through Amazon.com or another distributor. I have starred those that are currently unavailable for purchase and recommend trying to rent them or borrow them from a library.

Ashpet: an Appalachian Folktale. Directed by Tom Davenport, 1988.

Cinderella. Directed by Wilfred Jackson. Disney Studios, 1949.

Cinderella. Directed by Charles S. Dubin. Based on Rogers & Hammerstein's 1957 musical. Samuel Goldwyn, 1964.

Cinderella. Executive producer Shelley Duvall. Directed by Mark Cullingham. Written by Mark Curtiss & Rod Ash. Platypus Production, 1984.

Cinderfella. Directed by Jerry Lewis. Written by Frank Tashlin. Paramount, 1960.*

Cindy Eller. Directed by Lee Grant. 1985. *

Ever After. Directed by Andy Tennant. 1998.

The Glass Slipper. Directed by Charles Walters. Written by Helen Deutsch. 1955.

La Cenerentola.. A 1981 production of Gioacchini Antonio Rossini's opera with Frederica Von Stade at La Scala in Milan. (Other more recent productions of this opera are also available on video.)

Mutzmag: An Appalachian Folktale. Directed by Tom Davenport, 1993.

My Fair Lady. Directed by George Cukor. Produced by Herman Levin, from the Lerner and Loewe musical. Screenplay by Alan Jay Lerner. Warner Brothers, 1964.

Pretty in Pink. Produced and directed by John Hughes. Paramount, 1986.

Prince Cinders. Directed by Derek Hayes. 1994.

Pygmalion. Directed by Anthony Asquith & Leslie Howard. 1938.

The Tender Tale of Cinderella Penguin. Directed by Janet Perlman.

CINDERELLA RESEARCH

Aarne, Antti, and Stith Thompson. (1961). *The Types of the Folktale*. 2nd rev. ed. Folklore Fellows Communications no. 184. Helskinki: Academia Scientariarum Fennica.

Cox, Marian Roalfe. (1893). *Cinderella; 345 Variants*. London: David Nutt.

Dundes, Alan. (1988). *Cinderella: A Casebook*. Madison: The University of Wisconsin Press.

Moss, Joy F. (1990). Cinderella Tales: A Multicultural Experience. In *Focus on Literature: A Context for Literacy Learning*. Katonah, NY: Richard C. Owen, pp. 167-185.

Philip, Neil. (1988). *The Cinderella Story*. London: Penguin.

Rooth, Anna Birgitta. (1951). *The Cinderella Cycle*. Lund: C.W.K. Gleerup.

Sierra, Judy. (1992). *The Oryx Multicultural Folktale Series: Cinderella*. Phoenix: Oryx Press.

Tatar, Maria. (1992). *Off With Their Heads! Fairy Tales and the Culture of Childhood*. Princeton: Princeton University Press.

Zipes, Jack. (1987). *Don't Bet on the Prince: Contemporary Feminist Fairy Tales in North America and England*. New York: Routledge.

WEB SITES

The Cinderella Project University of Southern Mississippi
http://www-dept.usm.edu/~engdept/cinderella/cinderella.html

Cinderella Stories
http://www.acs.ucalgary.ca/~dkbrown/cinderella.html

Cinderella Main Page
Part of The SurLaLune Fairy Tale Pages
by Heidi Anne Heiner
http://members.aol.com/surlalune/frytales/cinderel/index.htm

Russell Peck's Annotated Cinderella Bibliography
http://www.ub.rug.nl/camelot/cinder/cinintr.htm

CHAPTER 4

RECOMMENDED ILLUSTRATED EDITIONS OF *ALICE IN WONDERLAND*

Unfortunately, it is likely that some of these editions are out of print. However, they can still be tracked down in used book stores, through rare book sellers, and online. The more variety you have in the classroom the more fun for your students!

Carroll, Lewis. (1985). *Alice's Adventures Underground*. Illustrated by the author. London: Pavilion Books Limited and the British Library.
This is a facsimile edition of the manuscript Lewis Carroll wrote for Alice Liddell. It is worth having on hand to compare to the later published version.

Carroll, Lewis. (1988). *Alice's Adventures in Wonderland*. Illustrated by Anthony Browne. New York: Knopf.
This is always one of my students' favorite editions. Browne is the author/illustrator of many well-known picture books such as *Gorilla*.

Carroll, Lewis. (1993). *Alice's Adventures in Wonderland*. Retold by David Blair. Illustrated by Graham Evernden. Philadelphia: Running Press.
This is a miniature edition that my students have enjoyed handling.

Carroll, Lewis. (1982). *Alice's Adventures in Wonderland*. Illustrated by Barry Moser. New York: Harcourt Brace Jovanovich.
The illustrations in this edition are all woodcuts. They are certainly very dark. Moser is the most adult-oriented of any illustrator in my collection.

Carroll, Lewis. (1989). *Alice's Adventures in Wonderland*. Illustrated by Arthur Rackham. London: William Heinemann Ltd.
Rackham was an illustrator in the early part of this century known for many classics such as *Cinderella*. He was the first prominent illustrator to try *Alice* after Tenniel, and some critics did not treat him kindly.

Carroll, Lewis. (1993). *Alice's Adventures in Wonderland.* Abridged and Illustrated by Tony Ross. London: Andersen Press.
Tony Ross is a popular British illustrator. These are very lively, appealing drawings.

Carroll, Lewis. (1988). *Alice's Adventures in Wonderland.* Illustrated by John Tenniel and Bessie Pease Gutmann. Children's Classics.
An inexpensive edition. Gutmann's Alice is very young and innocent-looking.

Carroll, Lewis. (1991). *Alice's Adventures in Wonderland.* A pop-up book illustrated by Jenny Thorne after Sir John Tenniel. New York: Dell Yearling.

Carroll, Lewis. (1988). *Alice's Adventures in Wonderland.* Illustrated by Justin Todd. London: Lynx.
My students like Todd's colorful full-page illustrations very much.

Carroll, Lewis. (1989). *Alice's Adventures in Wonderland and Through the Looking-glass.* Illustrated by Marketa Prachaticka. Chicago: Wellington Publishing.
These are beautiful, highly original drawings.

Carroll, Lewis. (2000). *The Annotated Alice: The Definitive Edition.* Illustrated by John Tenniel. Introduction and notes by Martin Gardner. New York: Norton.
This is an extremely useful text to have on hand. This definitive edition combines the notes of an earlier annotated edition, also by Gardner, along with notes from *More Annotated Alice,* and later notes he accumulated.

Carroll, Lewis. (1986). *The Complete Alice and The Hunting of the Snark.* Illustrated by Ralph Steadman. London: Jonathan Cape Ltd.
Difficult to find, but terrific. I bought this copy in England some years ago. Steadman is a cartoonist and his drawings are wild and witty.

Carroll, Lewis. (1990). *More Annotated Alice.* Illustrated by Peter Newell. Notes by Martin Gardner. New York: Random House.
A beautiful edition. The Newell drawings are delightful. His Alice is a sleek, long-haired child, very different from Tenniel's. The notes in this edition are also included in the definitive edition of *The Annotated Alice.*

Carroll, Lewis. (1966). *The Nursery "Alice."* Illustrated by John Tenniel. New York: Dover.
My students have always gotten a kick out of this, Lewis Carroll's own adaptation for very young children.

Carroll, Lewis. (1989). *The Ultimate Illustrated Alice's Adventures in Wonderland*. Compiled and arranged by Cooper Edens. New York: Bantam.
If you can only get a couple of different editions make this one of them. It is full of illustrations by many different artists. Gives a fine overview of all the different approaches to the illustration of this book.

Carroll, Lewis (1999). *Alice in Wonderland*. Illustrated by Lizbeth Zwenger. New York: North-South Books.
A very lovely version by an award-winning Austrian illustrator.

Carroll, Lewis (1998). *Alice's Adventures in Wonderland*. Illustrated with photographs by Abelardo Morell. New York: Dutton.
My students invariably adore this edition. Morell uses parts of Tenniel's illustrations to create a unique photographic vision of the story. The originality fascinates my students. I highly recommend this book as it provides a very different way of visually interpreting such a popular story.

Carroll, Lewis (1996). *Alice's Adventures in Wonderland* with paintings by Angel Dominquez. New York: Artisan.
This is another very popular illustrator among my students. Dominquez's illustrations are large, bold, and colorful.

Carroll, Lewis (1999). *Alice's Adventures in Wonderland*. Illustrated by Helen Oxenbury. Cambridge, MA: Candlewick Press.
This popular British children's book illustrator won the prestigious Carnegie Medal in 1999 (the British equivalent to our Caldecott medal) for this book. A little too tame for my taste, but well worth having in your classroom collection.

Carroll, Lewis. (1993). *Walt Disney's Alice in Wonderland*. New York: Mouse Works, Penguin Books.
One of many book versions of the film.

Goldberg, Whoopi. (1992). *Alice*. New York: Bantam Books.
This is a wild story based on Wonderland characters. Great illustrations.

Rayher, E. (1982). *Alice's Flip Book*. New York: Merrimack Publ. Corp.
A little flip book of the Cheshire Cat, disappearing and reappearing.

Sheppard, Nancy. (1992). *Alitji in Dreamland*. An aboriginal version of Lewis Carroll's *Alice's Adventures in Wonderland*. Illustrated by Donna Leslie. Berkeley: Ten Speed Press.
An aboriginal retelling with striking artwork.

RECOMMENDED VIDEOS

Walt Disney's Alice in Wonderland. Walt Disney Home Video. 1991.

Dreamchild. Directed by Gavin Millar. Written by Dennis Potter. MGM/UA Video. 1992.

RECOMMENDED REFERENCES

Bjork, Christina. (1993). *The Other Alice: The Story of Alice Liddell and Alice in Wonderland.*
Illustrated by Inga-Karin Eriksson. Translated by Joan Sandin. Stockholm: Raben & Sjogren.
An excellent source of information on the real Alice and Lewis Carroll.

Brown, Sally. (1997). *The Original Alice.* London: The British Library.
A charming small book that provides insights into the first handwritten version of the story.

Cohen, Morton N. (1995). *Lewis Carroll: A Biography.* New York: Knopf.
Currently, the definitive biography on Carroll by a very prominent scholar. Rather long, but useful to have on hand.

Edinger, Monica. (2000). "Adventuring with Alice" in the Riverbank Review.
This is an article I wrote that describes some of my classroom work with Alice.

Hacher, Michael. (1985). *The Tenniel Illustrations to the "Alice" Books.* Ohio State University Press.
For anyone especially interested in the Tenniel illustrations.

Hudson, Derek. (1976). *Lewis Carroll: An Illustrated Biography.* London: Constable.
A good biography of Lewis Carroll.

Stoffel, Stephanie Lovett. (1997). *Lewis Carroll in Wonderland: The Life and Times of Alice and her Creator.* New York: Abrams.
An excellent small book on Carroll.

Stoffel, Stephanie Lovett. *The Art of Alice in Wonderland.* New York: Smithmark.
A wildly designed book chock-full of illustrations. The text is interesting, but the book itself is great fun to simply browse through.

RECOMMENDED WEB SITES

The Many Faces of Alice
www.dalton.org./alice

The Lewis Carroll Home Page
http://www.lewiscarroll.org/carroll.html

Bed-Time Story Alice
http://the-office.com/bedtime-story/classics-aliceinwonderland.htm

CHAPTER 5

DIFFERENT ILLUSTRATED EDITIONS

Baum, L. Frank. (2000). *The Annotated Wizard of Oz: The Centennial Edition*. Introduction, notes, and bibliography by Michael Patrick Hearn. Illustrated by W.W. Denslow. New York: Norton.

————. (1960). Originally published in 1900. *The Wonderful Wizard of Oz*. Illustrated by W. W. Denslow. New York: Dover.

————. (1986). *The Wonderful Wizard of Oz*. Illustrated by Barry Moser. Berkeley, CA: University of California.

————. (1999). *The Wonderful Wizard of Oz: The Kansas Centennial Edition*. Illustrated by Michael McCurdy. Kansas: University Press of Kansas.

————. (1997). *The Wizard of Oz*. Illustrated by Charles Santore. New York: Random House.

————. (1996). *The Wizard of Oz*. Illustrated by Lizbeth Zwerger. New York: North-South Books.

————. (1988). *The Wizard of Oz*. Illustrated by Michael Hague. New York: Henry Holt.

BOOKS ABOUT OZ

Carpenter, Angelica Shirley and Jean Shirley. (1992). *L. Frank Baum: Royal Historian of Oz*. Minneapolis: Lerner Publications.

Eyles, Allen. (1985). *The World of Oz*. New York: Viking Penguin.

Glassman, Peter, ed. (2000). *Oz–The Hundredth Anniversary Celebration: The Hundredth Anniversary Celebration*. New York: HarperCollins.

Harmetz, Aljean. (1988). *The Making of the Wizard of Oz: Movie Magic and StudioPower in the Prime of MGM—And the Miracle of Production*. New York: Hyperion.

Rushdie, Salman. (1993). *BFI Film Classics: The Wizard of Oz*. London: British Film Institute.

Scarfone, Jay. (1999). *The Wizardry of Oz: The Artistry and Magic of the 1939 M-G-M Classic*. New York: Random House.

FILMS

The Wizard of Oz. Directed by Victor Fleming, 1939.

WEB SITES

The Wonderful Wizard of Oz Web Site
http://www.eskimo.com/~tiktok

Piglet Press's Oz Encyclopedia
http://www.halcyon.com/piglet

The International Wizard of Oz Club
http://www.ozclub.org

CHAPTER 6

PROFESSIONAL BOOKS

Lewis, Valerie V. and Walter Mayes. (1998*). Valerie & Walter's Best Books for Children: A Lively, Opinionated Guide*. New York: Avon.

Trelease, Jim. (1995). *The Read-Aloud Handbook*. New York: Penguin.

GREAT READ-ALOUDS

The following books are those that others and I have found to be sure-fire read-alouds hits with upper elementary students. Most of the novels are fairly short because I think read-alouds shouldn't be too long. This is because if any one child in the class isn't enjoying the book he or she will not have to live with it too long. For this reason I have not included any of J. K. Rowling's Harry Potter books here (you will find them in the next chapter) although I have known many teachers who have read them aloud with great enthusiasm.

Alexander, Lloyd. (1999.) *Gypsy Rizka*. New York: Dutton.

Avi. Illustrated by Brian Floca. (1995). *Poppy*. New York: Orchard Books.

Clements, Andrew. (1996). *Frindle*. New York: Simon & Schuster.

Cooper, Susan. (1995). *The Boggart*. New York: Margaret K. McElderry Books.

Curtis, Christopher Paul (1995). *The Watsons Go to Birmingham — 1963*. New York: Delacorte.

Dr. Seuss with some help from Jack Prelutsky and Lane Smith. (1998*). Hooray for Diffendoofer Day!* New York: Knopf.

Eager, Edgar. (1954). *Half Magic*. New York: Harcourt Brace Jovanovich.

Fleischman, Paul. (1991). *The Half-a-Moon Inn*. New York: Harper Trophy.

Fleischman, Sid. (1997). *The Whipping Boy*. New York: William Morrow.

Hesse, Karen. (1996). *The Music of Dolphins*. New York: Scholastic.

Horvath, Polly. (1999). *The Trolls*. New York: Farrar Straus & Giroux.

Kurtz, Jane. (1998). *The Storyteller's Beads*. San Diego: Harcourt Brace & Co.

Levine, Gail Carson. (1999). *Dave at Night*. New York: HarperCollins.

Naylor, Phyllis Reynolds. (1993). *The Grand Escape*. New York: Atheneum.

O'Brian, Robert. (1971). *Mrs. Frisby and the Rats of NIMH*. New York: Scholastic.

Paulsen, Gary. (1995). *Harris and Me*. New York: Yearling Books.

Peck, Richard. (1998). *A Long Way from Chicago*. New York: Dial.

Pullman, Philip. (1998). *Clockwork*. New York: Scholastic.

Sachar, Louis. (1998). *Holes*. New York: Random House.

Scieszka, Jon. (1995). Illustrated by Lane Smith. *Math Curse*. New York: Viking.

Spinelli, Jerry. (1990). *Maniac Magee*. New York: Little, Brown.

Woodruff, Elvira. (1997). *The Orphan of Ellis Island : A Time-Travel Adventure*. New York: Scholastic.

Wrede, Patricia. (1990). *Dealing with Dragons*. San Diego: Harcourt Brace Jovanovich.

WEB SITES

Reading Aloud —- Is it Worth It?
http://www.education-world.com/a_curr/curr213.shtml

Reading Aloud —- Are Students Ever Too Old?
http://www.education-world.com/a_curr/curr081.shtml

Trelease on Reading Home Page
http://www.trelease-on-reading.com/home.html

CHAPTER 7

REFERENCES

Thomas, Dylan. (1984). *The Collected Stories*. New York: New Directions Books.

GREAT INDEPENDENT READING BOOKS FOR UPPER ELEMENTARY STUDENTS

The following are novels that students in my classes of the last few years have especially enjoyed reading independently. I have also included titles that other teachers and librarians have told me their students especially enjoyed. In the case of an author who has several popular titles (e.g., J. K. Rowling) I have only given one title. I should also point out that while these recommendations are fiction, children also very much enjoy nonfiction. In particular, my students have enjoyed reading biographies of a range of historical and contemporary famous people.

Alexander, Lloyd. (1964). *The Book of Three*. New York: Holt, Reinhart and Winston.

Blume, Judy. (1972). *Tales of a Fourth Grade Nothing*. New York: Dutton.

Burnett, Frances. (1987). Illustrated by Tasha Tudor. *The Secret Garden*. New York: HarperCollins.

Cameron, Ann. (1998). *The Secret Life of Amanda K. Woods*. New York: Farrar Straus Giroux.

Cleary, Beverely. (1999). *Ramona's World*. New York: Morrow Junior.

Creech, Sharon. (1995). *Walk Two Moons*. New York: HarperCollins.

Curtis, Christopher Paul. (1999). *Bud, Not Buddy*. New York: Delacorte.

Cushman, Karen. (1994). *Catherine Called Birdy*. New York: Clarion.

Dahl, Roald. (1964). *Charlie and the Chocolate Factory*. New York: Knopf.

Enzensberger, Hans Magnus. (1998). *The Number Devil: A Mathematical Adventure*. New York: Henry Holt.

Erdrich, Louise. (1999). *Birchbark House*. New York: Hyperion.

Fitzhugh, Harriet. (1990). *Harriet the Spy*. New York: HarperTrophy.

Fletcher, Ralph. (1996). *Fig Pudding*. New York: Clarion.

Gantos, Jack. (1999). *Joey Pigza Swallowed the Key*. York: Farrar Straus Giroux.

Holm, Jennifer L. (1999). *Our Only May Amelia*. New York: HarperCollins.

Jacques, Brian. (1968). *Redwall*. New York: Avon.

Juster, Norton. (1988). Illustrated by Jules Feiffer. *The Phantom Tollbooth*. New York: Random House.

Konigsburg, E. L.. (1968). *From the Mixed-Up Files of Mrs. Basil E. Frankweiler*. New York: Atheneum.

L'Engle, Madeline. (1962). *A Wrinkle in Time*. New York: Dell Yearling.

Lewis, C. S. (1950). *The Lion, the Witch and the Wardrobe*. New York: Macmillan.

Lowry, Loise. (1990). *Number the Stars*. New York: Clarion.

Naylor, Phyllis Reynolds. (1991). *Shiloh*. New York: Dell.

O'Brien. Robert C. (1971). *Mrs. Frisby and the Rats of NIMH*. New York: Macmillan.

Paterson, Katherine. (1978). *The Great Gilly Hopkins*. New York: Crowell.

Paulsen, Gary. (1997). *Hatchet.* New York: Simon & Schuster.

Pullman, Philip. (1996). *The Golden Compass: His Dark Materials, Book One.* New York: Knopf.

Rogers, Mary. (1972). *Freaky Friday.* New York: Harper and Row.

Rowling, J. K. (1998). *Harry Potter and the Sorcerer's Stone.* New York: Scholastic.

Spinelli, Jerry. (1997). *Wringer.* New York: HarperCollins.

Steig, William. (1972). *Dominic.* New York: Farrar Straus Giroux.

Wrede, Patricia. (1990). *Dealing with Dragons.* San Diego: Harcourt Brace & Co.

Yolen, Jane. (1988). *The Devil's Arithmetic.* New York: Viking.

WEB SITES
Association for Library Service to Children (American Library Association) Awards Page (includes Newbery, Caldecott, Notables, and others.)
http://www.ala.org/alsc/awards.html#notable